Beyond the Bus Stop

180 Ways to Help Your Child Succeed in School

Robert E. Weyhmuller, Jr.
Illustrations by Stephen Stuart-Gibson

HEINEMANN
Portsmouth, NH

Heinemann
A division of Reed Elsevier Inc.
361 Hanover Street
Portsmouth, NH 03801–3912
http://www.heinemann.com

Offices and agents throughout the world

The author and publisher wish to thank those who have generously given permission to reprint borrowed material:

Cover from *American Girl* © Copyright 1998 by Pleasant Company. Reprinted by permission of Pleasant Company, 1-800-234-1278.

Photo of electronic dictionary courtesy of Seiko Instruments USA Inc.

Library of Congress Cataloging-in-Publication Data
Weyhmuller, Robert E.
    Beyond the bus stop : 180 ways to help your child succeed in
school / Robert E. Weyhmuller, Jr.
        p. cm.
    ISBN 0-325-00125-1 (alk. paper)
    1. Education—Parent participation. 2. Home and school.
I. Title. II. Title: 180 ways to help your child succeed in school.
LB1048.5.W49   1999
371.19'2—dc21   99-13991
                                                          CIP

Editor: Leigh Peake
Production: Elizabeth Valway
Illustrations: Stephen Stuart-Gibson
Cover design: Darci Mehall, Aureo Design
Manufacturing: Louise Richardson

Printed in the United States of America on acid-free paper
04   DA   4 5 6

Contents

Introduction

Success in school doesn't happen without parental support. Whether your son happily skips off to kindergarten or your daughter trudges down the hall to seventh-grade science class, your child needs your help to succeed in school.

I'm a special education teacher and learning disabilities consultant who has participated in nearly a thousand parent-teacher conferences over the past twenty-two years. I still cringe when a mother argues, "But she told me she does her homework in school," or a father complains, "He should be old enough to study on his own." Although there is a period of time when kids know it all (usually between the ages of thirteen and seventeen), children still need loving supervision and caring guidance at least until they toss their tassels at high school graduation.

I once waited at a traffic light behind a minivan displaying a bumper sticker proclaiming, "Mom's Taxi." I visualized a Wilma Flintstone–type mom, busily peddling her brood throughout the neighborhood, dropping young'uns off at the bowling alley, ball park, church hall, and youth center. A dutiful mother, the driver was no doubt proud of her responsibility to see her children happily engaged in recreational activities. But, I wondered, how much time had she spent at school that year, equally committed to ensuring her children's academic success?

You need to spend as much time in school talking with teachers as you spend at the baseball field or dance studio talking with coaches. You also need to make the same effort to see that your child is prepared for school, completes homework, and studies for tests. Don't misunderstand me, athletics and community activities are important, but education is your child's gateway to the future.

Because most schools are in session 180 days a year, I have compiled 180 ways for you to guarantee that your child triumphs in school. Many of the suggestions in this book come directly from the teachers, counselors, and parents who have joined with me over the years in helping kids do their best. Some suggestions are easily followed; others take more time, and perhaps more commitment, than operating Mom's Taxi. But if you start practicing them today, your child will succeed in school.

Read to Your Child Every Day

Children who read, succeed. Reading is the single most important skill a child needs in order to do well in school. And reading to your child every day is the single most important activity you can do to help your child become a better reader. Teachers have known it for years, and a study conducted by the U.S. Department of Education has shown that children whose parents read to them regularly are typically more successful in elementary school.

So when should you begin? The American Academy of Pediatrics recommends beginning when your baby is six months old. That's when my wife and I started reading to our son. As a teenager today, he's a good reader who loves books. But it's never too late to start. You can help your children succeed in school by reading aloud to them today.

Read to Your Child Every Day

1. Read aloud to your child.

It sounds like such a simple thing. But will reading to your child every day really help her succeed in school? The answer is emphatically, YES!

It's a fact. There's no better way to instill a love for reading in your child than by reading aloud to her. Children who are read to fall in love with books. They also develop good reading abilities earlier, become better listeners, and develop a stronger command of written language. But reading to your child every day does more than just feed the mind. It gives you and your child something special—it gives you together time.

Cuddle up with Chris Van Allsburg's *Polar Express* and feel the magic tingle your three-year-old. Explore Seymour Simon's *Wild Babies* and share the excitement of learning with your seven-year-old. Discover *There's a Boy in the Girls' Bathroom* by Louis Sachar and wipe tears of laughter from your ten-year-old's eyes. Befriend Gary Paulsen's *Nightjohn*, and suffer along with your fourteen-year-old when human injustice tears her apart.

Looking for some good books to read to your child? Here are some sources to help you:

Books for Children is a booklet published yearly by the Library of Congress, available through the U.S. Government Printing Office.

The New Read-Aloud Handbook by Jim Trelease. New York: Penguin Books, 1989.

The Latest and Greatest Read-Alouds by Sharron L. McElmeel. New York: Libraries Unlimited, Inc., 1994.

2. Read a textbook chapter together.

Children complain that textbooks are boring. One problem is that textbooks are written at or above grade level. Another problem is the concise writing style that textbook authors are forced to use. Coupled together, these make reading and comprehending textbooks difficult for some children.

You can improve your child's understanding of textbook material by reading aloud with fluency and expression. Giving further explanations and stimulating more talk about the subject is a surefire way of easing textbook boredom and piquing interest in the subject matter.

3. Read newspaper articles together.

Newspaper articles are good sources of information and generate great dinner table conversation. Pick up a newspaper and excite your child with adventure, war, mystery, romance, natural disasters, politics, and far away places. It's hard to find an excuse for not reading a newspaper to your child. Daily papers are inexpensive and local weeklies are often free. You can easily read a news article to your child and talk about it in one sitting.

Teachers at every grade level discuss current events in school. Your informed child will join class discussions and offer opinions after listening to newspaper articles.

4. Read favorite authors together.

Select several books by your child's favorite author. If your child hasn't discovered a favorite author yet, introduce him to some of these celebrities:

Betsy Byars
Beverly Cleary
Roald Dahl
Tomie DePaola
Don Freeman
Ezra Jack Keats
Steven Kellogg
Robert McCloskey
Jim Murphy
Peggy Paris

Gary Paulsen
Robert Newton Peck
Beatrix Potter
H. A. Ray
Louis Sachar
Maurice Sendak
William Steig
Chris Van Allsburg
Judith Viorst

5.

Get your child "hooked on reading" by finding books that explore their interests.

Does your child have a passion for polar bears, remote-controlled airplanes, or cheerleading? Find a book about your child's interest at your library and read it together.

Mention read-alouds and most people immediately think of fiction. But children's nonfiction can be breathtaking, heart-pounding, or simply beautiful.

Enjoy the beauty of Seymour Simon's *Wild Babies*:

> As big and powerful as giraffes are, they are very peaceful animals. A herd of giraffes on the move can look like a bunch of giant long-stemmed flowers flowing across the African plains.

Here's a firsthand account of a young Civil War soldier returning home, as told in Jim Murphy's *The Boys' War*:

I reached home May 25th 1865. I found my father and mother working in the garden. Neither knew me at first glance, but when I smiled and spoke to them, mother recognized me and with tears of joy clasped me to her arms. My father stood by gazing upon me in mute admiration. Their long-lost boy had been found.

6. Read humor books together.

Has your child heard any good jokes lately? Has he been riddled to tears this week? Did he have fun with puns this month? When was the last time he bounced on your belly, laughing out loud? Tickle your child's funny bone with a good humor book. It's a great way to shake the sillies out.

7. Read award-winners together.

Choose a Newbery Medal winner or an honor book. Awarded annually to the author of the most distinguished contribution to American literature for children, these books are easily identified by the gold or silver emblem on the front cover. Check out these winners of the past ten years:

1999   *Holes* by Louis Sachar. New York: Farrar, Straus, and Giroux

1998   *Out of the Dust* by Karen Hesse. New York: Scholastic

1997   *The View from Saturday* by E.L. Konigsburg. New York: Atheneum

1996   *The Midwife's Apprentice* by Karen Cushman. New York: Clarion Books

1995   *Walk Two Moons* by Sharon Creech. New York: HarperCollins

1994   *The Giver* by Lois Lowry. Boston: Houghton Mifflin

1993   *Missing May* by Cynthia Rylant. New York: Orchard Books

1992   *Shiloh* by Phyllis Reynolds Naylor. New York: Atheneum

1991   *Maniac Magee* by Jerry Spinelli. Boston: Little Brown and Co.

1990   *Number the Stars* by Lois Lowry. Boston: Houghton Mifflin

8. Read childhood favorites together.

While advertisements boast the oxymoron "The New Classics" in big-screen entertainment, the timeless classics still provide hours of reading enjoyment and years of memories.

Close your eyes and step back in time. Take yourself back to high school, back to seventh grade, to fourth grade, to kindergarten. Which favorite books do you remember? Chances are, the titles you enjoyed when you were young will please your own child today. That's what makes them timeless.

Buy your child a beautiful hardbound book for the holidays. Most parents cringe at the thought of spending twenty dollars for a hardbound, illustrated edition of a children's classic but will drop fifty bucks on amusement ride tickets without hesitation. The rides provide a few hours of fun but the book is treasured for a lifetime.

9. Read poetry books together.

Read to your child every day
A book of poems is sweet parfait
Words as pretty as Queen Anne's lace
Or a funny muse for a change of pace
Filled with lyrics that often rhyme
All guaranteed better than mine

Check out these books of verse for hours of reading pleasure:

A Light in the Attic by Shel Silverstein. 1981. New York: Harper and Row

If I Were in Charge of the World and Other Worries by Judith Viorst. 1984. New York: Atheneum

The Random House Book of Poetry for Children collected by Jack Prelutsky. 1983. New York: Random House

Side by Side: Poems to Read Together collected by Lee Bennett Hopkins. 1988. New York: Simon and Schuster

Sing a Song of Popcorn: Every Child's Book of Poems collected by Beatrice Schenk deRegniers. 1988. New York: Scholastic

Where the Sidewalk Ends by Shel Silverstein. 1974. New York: HarperCollins

10. Read and discuss good literature together.

You can help your child develop a deeper understanding of the book he is reading by reading it too and discussing it with him. Ratings soared when Oprah Winfrey started her televised Book Club, proving that people enjoy talking about good books.

Discussing theme, plot, character development, and author's purpose will enhance your child's reading and enable him to answer questions in class and on exams. An added bonus for you, besides being introduced to good literature, is having something enjoyable to talk about with your child.

11. Provide definitions for unknown words for your child as needed.

When reading with your child, tell her any word that she cannot identify immediately. Sending her to the dictionary or taking a long time to decode words interferes with comprehension and kills interest.

The purpose for reading *Peter Pan* is to analyze the implications of social rebellion of youth against authority.

I don't think so.

Always keep foremost in mind the reason why your child is reading. If she is reading to acquire information, don't allow her to stumble over unknown words to the point that comprehension is compromised. If the new word is an important vocabulary term, you can go back later and talk about it.

When your child is reading for enjoyment, keep the reading enjoyable. Lighten the load by supplying unknown words and by sharing the reading—every other chapter, or every other page, or every other paragraph—depending on your child's reading fluency.

12. Buy your child a magazine subscription.

Looking for a birthday present for your child? How about a magazine subscription? If you're not in tune with children's publications, ask your child's teacher or librarian. There are many superb magazines to spark your child's interest and motivate her reading.

Here is a list of some of my favorites. There are many more.

Title	Suggested Age Range
American Girl	7–11
Boys' Life	8–18
Breakaway	12–18
Brio	12–17
Chickadee	3–9
Child Life	9–11
Cobblestone	8–14
Contact Kids	8–14
Cricket	9–14
Disney Adventures	7–14
Dolphin Log	2–13
Guideposts for Kids	7–12
Highlights for Children	2–12
Humpty Dumpty's Magazine	4–6

13. Make your home a literature-rich environment.

Fill your home with books and magazines. Promote reading by letting your child catch you reading often.

Be a good role model. Children want to grow up to be "just like mommy" or "just like daddy." Show your child that reading is enjoyable by reading often. You'll be glad you did, and proud that your child grew up to be a reader, "Just like mommy or daddy."

14. Urge your child keep a record of every book he reads.

Three-by-five-inch index cards work well for this. Have your child record the title and author and the date he read the book and a few sentences telling about it. Keeping an index file is a great way for him to revisit old literary friends and recommend favorite books to others.

15. Allow your child to stay up an extra thirty minutes provided she is reading.

Whether your child sneaks under the covers with a flashlight or sits comfortably on the living room sofa, what better reason to stay up a little past bedtime than reading? By making reading a special privilege, you show your child that books are highly valued in your home. And when reading becomes a treat instead of a chore, your child will more likely discover the joy of reading. So, allow your child to break curfew once or twice a week, provided she is reading, and both of you will find pleasure in breaking the rules.

16. Celebrate your child's birthday by giving a book to the class.

By donating a book to the classroom library in her name, your child will learn the joy of giving and win the admiration of her teacher and classmates.

Many teachers stockpile books and magazines for their students to use during silent reading time or for take-home recreational reading. Here's a way that your child can contribute to a good cause.

Two weeks before her birthday, tell your child to look through her teacher's lending library to see which books are in stock. Then venture on down to your local bookstore together to buy a title that the teacher doesn't own. Your child might choose a personal favorite, a nonfiction book linked to her grade-level curriculum, or the latest Newbery winner. Before gift wrapping the present, have your child inscribe the inside front cover:

To Ms. _____'s class on my birthday.
From (your child's name)
Full date (to mark her birthday)

Your child will be fondly remembered for years to come.

17. Spend an hour browsing a bookstore together.

While I perused the children's literature shelves, my pre-teenage son checked out the course offerings at the United States Air Force Academy in an encyclopedic text that weighed more than he did. Pausing briefly to enjoy the irony, I quickly returned to the majesty of Robert Sabuda's *Tutenkamen's Gift*. It was a rainy Sunday afternoon. The public library was closed, but Borders was open for business, providing an opportunity to read with my child, every day.

18. Check out your local library.

Where else can your child safari with Siberian tigers, swim the Pacific with humpback whales, dazzle in the brilliance of deep-water tropical fish, and wander the expanses of outer space? Take your child to the library at least once every two weeks.

Libraries have books, magazines, audiotapes, and videos. Libraries also have atmosphere. They smell musty old and printer's-ink new. They are bright horizons whose towering bookshelves stretch to the ceiling. They are dark, secret places with endless book-lined passageways. Libraries are child-innocent, with huge stuffed animals and warm, carpeted reading circles. Libraries are scholarly chic, with green computer monitors and clicking mechanical printers.

Most libraries sponsor children's programs throughout the school year and during the summer months. So, check out your local library with your child, and make sure she has her own library card to open new horizons.

19.

After reading a book, watch the movie together.

Authors are word geniuses. Yet, no matter how descriptive they paint their scenes or how detailed they develop their characters, the reader's own imagination unleashes the magic of books. Hollywood may have special effects, but a child's mind knows no boundaries. So, read a book with your child, and then watch the movie. Chances are you'll both find that you liked the book better.

20.   Buy age-appropriate stationery for your child.

Children today don't have many opportunities to write, yet writing is a complex process requiring practice. Your child can get more practice by having legitimate reasons to write. Keeping in touch with a friend from summer camp or writing a thank-you note to Grandpop provides the perfect opportunity. But kids are turned off by large sheets of blank paper. And notebook paper screams of schoolwork.

The solution is to buy attractive stationery. Letter paper and note cards are small, so less writing fills a page. Fun graphics and matching envelopes make writing and sending notes even more enjoyable.

21. Help your child find a pen pal.

Writing on paper still carries expectations of proper spelling, grammar, and punctuation, while e-mail is very casual :) Your child will write more frequently, knowing his letters are read by a friend. Establishing a pen pal sets up a routine of sending and receiving correspondence, and few things please children more than receiving personal mail. Another advantage is that letters may be stored in a shoe box and retrieved years later, while e-mail is simply deleted :(

So where do you find a pen pal for your child? Start with people you know. Do you have an out-of-state cousin with children similar in age to yours? How about business acquaintances? Teachers often network with other teachers to start pen pal relationships, so ask your child's teacher. Magazines may be another source. *Home Education* runs a pen pal connections column each month.

22. Encourage your child to write a letter to the local newspaper editor.

Is a hot topic being debated in your town? Nothing is more rewarding for a youngster than seeing his work in print.

Any topic that gets your child's blood boiling is perfect to write about. Will a defeat of the school budget eliminate the music program? Did city council nix a new playground? Is the local pond too polluted to fish? Writing a letter to the editor provides a perfect opportunity for your child to get involved in his community and, at the same time, practice authentic writing. Just remind your young activist that the editor won't make corrections, so he should revise and proofread his letter before mailing it.

23. Teach your child to use strong verbs.

Simas Kaselionis once said, "Writers aren't like mushrooms—you can't grow them." Maybe not, but you can nurture them, and teach them a few good tricks.

Back in the dark ages when I attended school, teachers taught us to polish our compositions with adjectives. "The sad little boy went down the long, tree-lined street looking for his lost black and white dog." Like fine jewelers, we crafted our sentences by stringing adjectives like pearls on a necklace. But a dozen pearls, though gracious, do not match the brilliance of a single diamond.

Strong verbs, like diamonds, radiate a brilliance that makes sentences shine. Instead of punctuating sentences with adjectives, teach your child to use strong verbs. Avoid forms of the verb *be* (*is, am, are, was, were*) and other helping verbs, such as *could, would, shall, do, did, does*. Instead of "Aubrey is happy," try "Aubrey cartwheeled across the living room floor." Replace "Luke was hungry" with "Luke gulped down three hot dogs."

With practice, your young author will be penning gems like this: "Heartbroken, Tyrone plodded the endless street searching for his lost beagle."

24. Combat writer's block by talking together.

Even great authors occasionally suffer from writer's block, so why should your child be any different? Help her get started on a writing assignment by doing what comes naturally—talking.

The four components of language are reading, writing, listening, and speaking. We receive information through reading and listening and express information through writing and speaking. So when your child has difficulty expressing herself in writing, prod her expressive language through talk.

Generate topic discussions by asking who, what, when, where, why, and how. After five or six minutes of talking, tell your child to jot down key words or phrases on scratch paper. Then help her organize her thoughts into a logical sequence of beginning, middle, and end. She can do this by simply numbering the key words in the order she wants to write about them. Then leave her alone. Come back in twenty minutes to check her progress.

25. Practice handwriting separately.

It's difficult for young children to achieve good penmanship while generating ideas and concentrating on sentence structure and grammar. Writing is a complex process. It involves eye-hand coordination, letter formation, spelling, grammar, syntax, organization of thoughts, creativity, patience, and persistence.

Handwriting is formally taught in school in kindergarten through third or fourth grade. After that, teachers assume that most children know the mechanics of letter formation and turn their instruction to the process of written language. You can help your six- to nine-year-old improve his penmanship by practicing handwriting as a separate activity. Here are some tips:

- Buy thick crayons and pencils. They're easier for young children to grasp. Triangular rubber pencil grips also help.

- Provide long pencils with sharp points. Pencils are cheap.

- Always use lined paper. Darkening the lines with a felt-tipped marker may help.

- Remember that ergonomics are important for kids, too. Provide a table and chair at the proper height for your youngster. Make sure the work space is smooth, uncluttered, and well lit.

- Suggest making lists. It's easier to practice single words, rather than long sentences. And children enjoy listing collections of toys, audiotapes, dolls, friends, etc.

- Make it real. Children want to make a good impression. Encourage your child to send short greetings, invitations, and thank-you notes.

- Encourage copying and tracing. Young children might trace picture outlines before coloring. Older children can copy spelling words.

- Give praise. Say something positive about your child's writing.

26. Encourage neatness for final drafts.

Your child's final written work should present an overall neat appearance and be legible. Neatness does count, and usually nets higher grades.

Do erasures make Swiss cheese of your child's paper? Do "straight" lines look more like inchworms crawling around the page? Do you need a cryptologist to decipher your child's handwriting? Sloppiness usually occurs when children rush through their work, are frustrated, or are tired. So, schedule homework time to avoid all three.

Neatness may not come naturally to your child, but you can teach him to be a neater student. Insist that he use a ruler to draw lines and always use a pencil for math. When transitioning from pencil to pen for writing assignments, buy your child erasable ink pens.

Redo is a four-letter word, but sometimes necessary. English teachers often encourage their students to work on a "sloppy copy" of a developing writing piece, making the children fully aware from the start that they will rewrite the final draft. Although this may not be necessary for next-day homework assignments, you should make it the rule for long-term reports.

27. Remember that writing and reading go hand in hand.

Your child will become a better writer when she reads extensively. It really does make sense when you think about it. When your child reads, she is focusing on correct spelling, punctuation, sentence structure, paragraph development, and the overall organization of the complete text. She is also observing style and voice.

Can you imagine anyone learning to write poetry without reading poetry? Children also learn to write narrative, expository, and persuasive text by reading these forms of writing.

28. Drill math facts the old-fashioned way—with flash cards.

Your child will have a real advantage over his classmates when he spouts off math facts with the precision of Robbie the Robot. Memorizing facts enables children to complete worksheets, homework, and tests quickly and accurately, thus earning higher grades. 9 + 7 = 16. Period. End of thinking. It's a fact. When children count on their fingers, they make mistakes. They lose track or count incorrectly.

Use flash cards to teach your child addition, subtraction, multiplication, and division facts. Here's how:

- Buy or make your flash cards.
- Drill your child every night with the cards.
- Put every fact card your child knows automatically in one pile.
- When he stumbles or doesn't know a fact, put that card in another pile.
- Keep the piles separated with rubber bands.
- Review the unknown facts nightly.
- When a fact is mastered, place it in the "known" pile.

Both you and your child will be delighted to see the "known" pile grow and the "unknown" pile shrink.

29. Make sure your child knows multiplication facts by fourth grade.

Drill and repetition are the best ways to help your child learn multiplication facts. The good news is there are dozens of opportunities during the week to practice and there are many ways of doing it.

Flash cards do work. You can make your own by cutting three-by-five-inch index cards in half and writing one fact on each card. Use the cards whenever you have spare time at home. You can also practice in the car by calling out facts, or by asking your child to recite the answers to the times tables: 4, 8, 12, 16, 20, 24, 28, 32, 36, 40, 44, 48. Whenever possible, keep it light—make it into a game. Learning is easy when it's fun.

30. Challenge your child with mental math problems.

Mental math comes in handy on tests, at the cashier's counter, in restaurants, in the kitchen, and at the workbench. Help your child develop mental math skills with word problems like "Jack has $20 and spends $13 at the arcade. How much money does he have left?" Or multiple calculation problems like "6 times 5, plus 3, minus 4, equals . . ." You can use mental math problems while waiting in the doctor's lounge, cooking dinner, or walking through the mall.

31.

Teach your child liquid and dry measurement by cooking together.

The relationship among teaspoon, tablespoon, ounce, cup, pint, and quart is best learned through real-life application—in the kitchen, of course. Satisfy your child's appetite for learning measurement by blending a sauce, making a stew, or baking a cake together.

32. Help your child develop a sense of time and distance.

How long is the school day? How far is it to grandmother's house? What is the distance around the earth at the equator?

To be good in mathematics, children must develop quantitative thinking. They need to make judgments about shapes, amounts, sizes, time, and distance. This is what I call developing a "math sense." A twelve-year-old who states that 500,000 fans packed the football stadium doesn't have good quantitative thinking when it comes to amounts. Nor does the five-year-old who says it takes about ten hours to walk to the neighborhood food store.

You can help your child develop quantitative thinking by giving him strategies to estimate, judge, compare, and contrast. Knowing how many seats the average stadium holds, how long it takes to walk a mile, and how far it is to the store will enable him to make judgments about relationships among these variables.

33. Teach your child to use a ruler and measure to the quarter inch.

Children need to measure distances accurately and estimate length, width, and height of objects. But few math curriculums devote much time teaching how to use a ruler. In the United States, children in elementary school need to measure accurately to the quarter inch. Older children should be able to measure to a sixteenth of an inch.

Although the "Think Metric" movement never gained much momentum in the United States, teachers still require students to exchange inches for centimeters in science lab, forcing children to learn two systems.

Take your child on a measuring spree around the house and have fun measuring everything from the TV screen to the bedroom carpet. While you're at it, teach your child how to estimate. A good trick is to learn the size of standard objects and use them to approximate length. Notebook paper is $8\frac{1}{2}$ x 11 inches. Computer disks are $3\frac{1}{2}$ x $3\frac{5}{8}$ inches. Floor tiles in most classrooms are 12 x 12 inches, and new wooden pencils are $7\frac{1}{2}$ inches long.

Pop Quiz: How long is a 3 x 5 index card?

34. Teach your child to highlight key math words and symbols.

Buy your child a set of highlight markers. Teach him to highlight key direction words on papers and tests (but not in textbooks without permission). Key words might include *sum, difference, all together, estimate, factor, volume, area, graph.*

This technique is particularly helpful for children who have difficulty following written directions or for those who cannot focus their attention on text. If your child gets confused when addition, subtraction, and multiplication problems are mixed together on the same math page, here's the solution to his problem. Teach him to highlight the operation signs in different colors (e.g., yellow for +, blue for –, pink for x). Then, instruct him to complete the problems while paying close attention to the highlighted operation signs.

35. Help your child develop common sense.

Sometimes called logical thinking, this helps not only in math, but also in science, social studies, and even on the playground.

A new suit, regularly priced at $240.00, is on sale at 10 percent off. How much will the suit cost? If your child answers $24.00 or $2,400, she hasn't used common sense. Likewise, if your child walks in front of a swing or under a seesaw, her lack of common sense may deliver her a bump on the noggin.

36. Help your child learn to solve word problems.

Word problems are to students what income taxes are to adults. Kids know they'll get into a heap of trouble if they don't do them, but they can't figure out where to begin.

Begin by reading the problem to your child. Draw a picture or diagram of it. Highlight or underline all numbers. Be careful—some numbers are hidden (e.g., *dozen, foot, year, twice as much*). Ask your child if he thinks the answer will be a larger number or smaller number. Then determine which operation to perform (addition or multiplication for larger whole-number answers; subtraction or division for smaller answers). Identifying key words, such as *sum, all, total, how many are left,* will also signal which operation to choose. If your child is still stuck, a good trick is to substitute smaller numbers for the ones in the problem. Now, ask your child to solve the problem and check his math with a calculator.

37.
Put homework first on your child's "Things to Do" list.

Your child won't be successful in school if scouts, gymnastics, cheerleading, soccer, and a part-time job come first and homework is squeezed in if time permits.

As the driver of "Mom's (or Dad's) Taxi," you're in control. It's up to you to see that school doesn't take a backseat to your child's education. You'll know you've crossed the center line when your child hasn't enough time to complete homework, when she has more than two after-school activities on a given day of the week, and when she starts seeing the gas station attendant more frequently than her friends.

Your teenager's after-school job is like a learner's permit. It gives her an opportunity to experience an adult activity, but with restrictions. Some limits are governed by child labor laws, but others will be imposed by you. Your teen spends about thirty-five hours per week at her full-time job—school. She should spend no more than half of that amount of time per week working at an after-school job.

38. Establish a homework routine.

Decide with your child on a time each night to do homework, and stick to it.

Teachers set up a classroom routine because children like routine. It gives them comfort and stability. Kids like knowing when things will happen, rather than being caught off guard. If you suddenly call your child in from his outside play to start homework, chances are you will meet more resistance than the allied forces on D-Day. But if you establish a routine, such as homework begins at 5:00 P.M., arguments will be greatly reduced.

39. Provide your child with a comfortable place to do homework.

This doesn't have to be hospital sanitary or library quiet. Some children work fine lying on the floor; others need a desk. Music is okay if it's not distracting. TV is out.

HOMEWORK ?

40.
Make sure supplies are available where your child does homework.

Chances are your child will need to use pencils, scissors, crayons, colored paper, and rulers on a steady basis. These should be kept together, either in a desk drawer, shoe box, or other convenient location.

Homework takes a lot longer when your child wastes time searching the house for needed supplies. If possible, purchase inexpensive materials for your child's own use. (More expensive items, such as dictionaries, can be shared.) Children take pride in ownership and take better care of personal school supplies. When your child has all needed supplies at hand, she will appreciate being able to work efficiently, and you will appreciate fewer requests to find misplaced materials.

41. Save old magazines to provide pictures for homework.

Help your child collect an array of old magazines from friends and relatives for cutting out pictures. Her collection should include gardening, nature/environment, history, news, food, crafts, and women's magazines.

It's nine o'clock at night and your child is about to wrap up her last assignment, "Cut out five pictures that depict success." You scour the house looking for magazines but your only find is the *TV Guide* and *National Geographic*, which your spouse maintains in pristine condition. Do you . . .

- a. throw on a jacket over your PJs and dash out to the drugstore
- b. curse out the teacher for giving such a stupid assignment
- c. curse yourself out for not keeping a collection of old magazines in the house
- d. all of the above

Keeping a collection of old magazines on hand not only helps your child succeed with her homework assignment, but also eliminates a potential homework hassle for you.

42.

Keep reference books within arm's reach of the place where your child does homework.

Most likely, your child will need to use a dictionary, a thesaurus, and an encyclopedia on a regular basis. Picture this scenario:

Your child darts down the steps on her way to retrieve the dictionary, when suddenly Bart Simpson reaches out from the small screen, kidnapping her. Escape takes fifteen minutes. Now, edging past the refrigerator, your child is attacked by a chicken leg, left over from Tuesday's supper. Fighting down to the bare bone, she rises triumphant, and parades into the family room. Hypnotized by Fido's sad eyes, she stoops to give a loving pat. The dictionary on the bookshelf is finally within arm's reach. And homework just took twenty-five minutes longer to complete.

43. Buy an age-appropriate dictionary for your child.

Unless your nine-year-old is reading John Milton, don't buy him a collegiate dictionary. Buy one that he can read. He'll use it more.

Here's a dictionary quiz using *Random House Webster's College Dictionary*, 1991 edition. I'll give the definition, you supply the word:

1. a description or explanation, as of a process, illustrated by examples, specimens, or the like.
2. the science of calculating by diagrams.
3. the enveloping or outer part of anything, especially when dry or worthless.
4. a space in which something, as a part of a mechanism, can move.

(Answers can be found upside down at the bottom of the next page.)

A dictionary can be a useful tool or an object of frustration. To be a useful tool for your child, it must be easy to read with clear definitions. There are many excellent dictionaries on the market today for elementary and junior high school students. An eight-hundred-page book with full color art, fairly large text, and clear definitions will set you back about $17.00.

Electronic dictionaries are faster and easier to use than print dictionaries and work much like computer spellcheckers and thesauruses, although definitions may be less clear. Look for one that provides choices for misspelled entries. Teach your child to use an electronic dictionary, and you may never be asked how to spell a word again.

Answers to dictionary quiz on page 49: 1. demonstration, 2. graphics, 3. husk, 4. play

44. Buy a three-hole paper punch and a sturdy binder for all those loose papers that come home and must return to school.

Children love losing loose assignment papers and skill pages more than teachers love lending them out. Fortunately, children also love punching holes in paper, which makes this little trick a real winner.

45.

Check with your child's teacher before correcting homework.

Some teachers grade homework based on correctness, while others use homework to identify areas of difficulty that need more teaching. You may be doing your child more harm than good by correcting all of her papers before the teacher sees them.

It's always a good idea to let the teacher know exactly where your child is having trouble. A brief note attached to the homework paper can get your child extra help immediately.

Dear Mrs. Rodriquez,

Cindy Lou still doesn't know how to do subtraction with regrouping. Can you go over this again with her?
Thanks,

Mr. McDonald

46. Before your child gets started, spend a few minutes asking questions about homework assignments.

"Is the assignment clear? Which directions need more explanation? How do you plan to proceed with this assignment? How long do you think it will take to complete this report?"

Taking a little time before starting homework to clarify directions and devise an action plan can save hours of frustration. Imagine your child's balking when he discovers that he needed to write only five sentences, instead of five paragraphs, or that the instructions said to calculate only the odd-numbered problems.

47. Turn off the TV during homework time, even if your child studies in another room.

This helps prevent the mad rush to get homework done just to watch sitcom reruns.

It's unfair to expect your child to be doing homework while someone else in the house is watching television. You might get away with it if CNN is on, but most children find it impossible to tune out the tube.

Rather than have your child rush through homework in order to watch a favorite show, you might consider working around the program. Allow your child to take a break to watch the show, and then turn off the TV and resume homework.

Television is the most distracting force in the universe.
—Bob Weyhmuller

48. Avoid a major homework hassle by instructing your child to do the first few problems or answer the first few questions and then give them to you to check.

It's far less frustrating to redo two problems than a whole page.

Nothing makes a kid go ballistic faster than telling her to redo her homework. First, you've insulted her by saying she's wrong, and second, she must spend twice as long working at an already unpleasant task.

By staying nearby when your child begins a new homework assignment, you can ward off potential explosions by making certain she gets off to a smooth start.

49. Unless your child is in kindergarten, if he says he doesn't have homework (or that he did it in school) three days in a row, call the teacher.

You must be vigilant on this one. Here's what you need to remember:

FACT: Teachers give homework.

FACT: Teachers give homework four or five nights a week.

FACT: Teachers do not give students time to complete homework in school. (Why do you think it's called HOMEwork?)

FACT: Teachers do check daily that homework is completed.

FACT: Students do not complete homework in study hall.

FACT: Students do not complete homework on the bus.

FACT: Students who occasionally complete homework in school or at a friend's house have no problem when their parents check that it's done correctly.

FACT: Students who regularly do not complete homework earn lower report card grades.

50. Require that your child keep a homework assignment book, and check it nightly. You might get flack on this one, but it's critical.

If your child argues he can remember his assignments without writing them down, point out that you keep an appointment calendar and even lawyers would forget their briefs if it weren't for their secretaries.

Drug stores and office supply stores are chock-full of attractive assignment books and student calendars. Help your child select one appropriate for his grade level. Then insist he use it every day.

In order for your child to succeed in school, he must complete assignments on time. As a parent, you should have zero tolerance for your child's not knowing his assignments. Most teachers, throughout all grades, write homework on the chalkboard. Most kids have a thousand excuses for not writing it down, "The teacher didn't give us time . . . She forgot to write it on the board . . . I'm smart. I can remember." But kids don't remember, and many homework wars are fought not over how to do the work, but over what work needs to be done.

Try these suggestions to get your child into the routine of using an assignment book:

1. Check the assignment book nightly. Point out that it's a tool to use, just as pencils, erasers, and textbooks are tools.
2. Use positive reinforcement: "Thanks for using your assignment book. It really helps me understand what you need to do tonight."
3. Give a reward. "Because you wrote down your assignments each night this week, we'll have ice cream sundaes for dessert."
4. Give a consequence. "Forgetting your assignment book is not acceptable. We'll go back to school now and get it."

51.

Check in periodically during homework time to make sure your child is focused and on task.

At work, I have a supervisor. She's not there to bug me. Her job is to see that I do my job. Now, I'm a fairly responsible person with more than twenty years' experience. So why do I need a supervisor? Chances are, unless you're self-employed, you have a supervisor too. If adults need supervisors to oversee that their work is done correctly and on schedule, then why wouldn't children need a supervisor to do the same?

Every day I hear parents argue that their child should be old enough to do homework on his own. There seems to be a break in the logic here. Parents become frustrated after their child has spent hours in his room supposedly doing homework, only to find that the work isn't done or that it is done incorrectly. Avoid this frustration by supervising homework.

Depending on your child's age, check in with him every fifteen to thirty minutes. Don't bug him. Just ask what he has completed, and check that it's done correctly. If work is proceeding smoothly, be a good supervisor and leave. That way, nobody gets bugged.

52. Monitor homework even when you're not home.

Until corporate America gets in sync with the school calendar and businesses close their doors at 3:00 P.M., your older child may be on her own to start homework while you're at work. But don't fret. All you need is access to a telephone to keep your child on task. Here's what to do.

Establish a specific time for your child to begin homework. Call her fifteen minutes after the scheduled time to check that she has started her work. Review what assignments need to be done and approximate how long homework will take. Call again later to see if she is finished. Before hanging up, tell her you love her (even if she isn't finished, yet).

53. Don't take over projects.

Have you ever attended an elementary school science fair and stood gawking at a kindergartner's model of a rain forest, complete with soap-carved animals and hand-painted silk plants? Ask your child's teacher how much you should help with projects. There is a delicate balance between helping your child and doing the work for him.

It's hard not jumping in. All those projects we hated doing as kids now seem like such fun. And we can make them look much more attractive than our child can. But whose project is it, anyway? Hands-on projects provide excellent learning experiences, but you must give your child the experience. So, resist the urge—give guidance, but let your child have the fun.

54. Mark due dates for long-term projects on the calendar and help your child work toward completion at a steady pace.

Long-term projects drive families crazy because students procrastinate, putting off the assignment until the last possible moment. When a child announces on Saturday that her science project is due on Monday, parents go ballistic—and rightfully so. Here's how to avoid the bombshell.

Have your child mark her calender, indicating the date the assignment was announced by the teacher and the date it is due. Count the number of days between these two dates. Divide this number into fourths. Let's say the teacher gave the children twenty-four days to complete the assignment. Twenty-four divided by four equals six. Your child will mark her calendar every six days. For a project involving crafts and construction, proceed as follows:

On her calendar, your child counts six days after the assigned date and writes RESEARCH COMPLETED. She counts another six days and writes ALL MATERIALS BOUGHT OR COLLECTED. She counts another six days and writes PROJECT HALF-COMPLETED. Looking ahead to the day preceding the due date, she writes PROJECT FINISHED. Meet with your child on each of the indicated dates to make certain she is proceeding as planned.

A calendar for a written research report might look like this:

March

Sun	Mon	Tue	Wed	Thur	Fri	Sat
		1	2	3	4	5
6	7 *Report Assigned*	8	9	10	11	12
13 *Complete Research*	14	15	16	17	18	19 *Complete 1st draft*
20	21	22	23	24	25 *Complete 2nd draft*	26
27	28	29 *Put report in bookbag* 30		31 *Report Due*		

55. Resist the urge to hand your child an encyclopedia as a first source for research projects.

Instead, choose children's books from the library. They are easy to read, beautifully illustrated, and contain more in-depth information.

I have a personal bias against children researching from encyclopedias. First, they're rather boring, with text that's difficult for children to comprehend. Second, most students plagiarize them. They copy word-for-word with little understanding of what they are writing. Your child will learn more about the topic when she gathers information from children's nonfiction books. But don't discard that set of encyclopedias just yet. Look up the topic and study the subheadings that appear in the article. Use the subheadings to help organize the research report.

56.

Try using graph paper for messy math calculations.

Putting one digit in each square keeps numbers properly aligned. This works well for addition, subtraction, multiplication, and division. Another trick is to turn notebook paper sideways, so that the blue lines form columns. Believe me, no teacher will complain about cockeyed paper when numbers are aligned and answers are correct.

57. Have your child choose a partner to bring homework during an illness.

When the cold and flu season strikes, be prepared. Have your child choose an absentee partner—a reliable classmate to bring home assignments and books. Your child can do the same for her.

When your child is ill, she needs plenty of rest. But when she begins recuperating, both you and she will appreciate having something constructive to fill her day.

Plan ahead. Ask a classmate to bring home:

- textbooks
- workbooks
- worksheets
- classroom reading assignments
- homework assignments

If you expect your child will be home for several days, call her teacher. Ask him to clarify assignments. Also ask to borrow any videos he has shown during your child's absence. When your child returns to school, she'll be caught up with the rest of the class.

58.

If your child is spending too much time on homework each night, talk to the teacher.

Your child should not be spending more than two hours on homework in elementary school or three hours in junior high school. If so, perhaps you and the teacher can agree that after a reasonable amount of time, you will sign your child's work and he can put his books away.

The purpose of assigning homework is to:

- reinforce skills or concepts learned in class
- build students' ability to work independently
- give parents firsthand knowledge about what is being taught in school
- provide parents with a means of assessing their child's scholastic progress

Homework is like prescription medicine: The right dosage is beneficial but an excess can be deadly (or, at least, counter-productive).

If you feel your child is spending too much time doing home-work, check with other parents of children in your child's class. Determine if it's just your child, or if the teacher is being excessive. Whatever you determine, talk with the teacher and work out a plan satisfactory to both of you.

59.

Take a homework break to exercise with your child.

Physical exercise does as much good for the mind as it does for the body. A fifteen-minute walk with your child will help you both think more clearly.

60.

Don't neglect your child's need for help because you feel she should be able to do it alone.

This applies to copying assignments, completing homework, and remembering schedules. If she were old enough, she'd be doing it.

I remember being outraged that my three-year-old wasn't potty trained, until a social worker friend set my thinking straight, "Relax, Bob. I've never yet seen a kid enter kindergarten wearing diapers."

Sure, you want your child to mature into a responsible person. But, contrary to popular belief, if you throw a non-swimmer into a lake, chances are, she'll drown. If, in your impatience for maturity, you tell your child to sink or swim, chances are, she'll sink. You need to teach responsibility gradually. Guide your child step by step, and—eventually—she'll be swimming freestyle.

61. Know your limitations.

If the two of you are continuously facing off on the homework battlefield, find someone who can work with your child. This might be a high school student, an uncle, or a paid tutor.

Let's face it, some people just can't work together. Sure, you love your child and he loves you. But when the two of you dig in and draw your lines on the homework front, SCUD missiles begin flying.

What's the problem? Sometimes it's anger. Your child is angry because he has homework and can't go outside to play. You're angry because he's angry and you'd rather be anywhere except stuck on his hip doing homework.

Sometimes it's frustration. Your child is challenged by the work and frustrates easily. In turn, you're frustrated that he struggles so much.

Sometimes it's adolescence—that time in a youngster's life when he realizes that grown-ups don't know anything. So, no matter what you say, you're wrong.

Whatever the reason, if you can't help your child with homework, find someone who can. Life at home will be more pleasant, and your child will come away with something other than battle scars.

62. Learn the teacher's routine.

Are spelling words given on Monday and tested on Friday? Is there a test at the end of every social studies chapter? Knowing the routine enables you to help your child be prepared.

Contrary to popular belief, not all tests are given on Fridays. But most teachers do establish a routine and stick to it throughout the school year. By knowing the routine, you can guarantee your child is prepared for almost every test.

Speaking of tests, insist that your child brings home every test, for two reasons. The first is obvious. You must know your child's grade. The second is to help her do well on other tests.

Teachers, like most people, are creatures of habit. They not only follow a routine for giving tests, but also for the kinds of tests they give. Examine a social studies test, for example. If the teacher routinely gives ten multiple-choice questions and ten fill-in-the-blanks, practice these kinds of questions at home. If matching is included, you might help your child study by making up your own matching test.

63. Begin to study at least three days before the exam.

Insist that your child write scheduled test dates in his homework assignment book. Plan to study with him each night, for at least three nights, to prepare for the exam. Playing games makes studying less tedious. Try science jeopardy or vocabulary bingo. Games like "Beat the Clock" and "Password" develop automaticity. Remember, active studying is far more rewarding than passive studying.

64. Practice spelling words every night.

If your child has trouble learning spelling words, divide the list into four groups. Study the first group Monday night. Study the second group Tuesday night and review the first group. Study the third group on Wednesday and review the other two groups. Study the last group on Thursday and review all other words.

When children break down studying into manageable bits, and review nightly, they enjoy better grades on Friday's test.

65. Pretest your child's spelling on paper.

Except for an occasional spelling bee, spelling is a written, not an oral, task. Pretest your child's spelling by insisting that she write the words on paper rather than spell them orally.

Does your child recite every word perfectly on Thursday night but bomb Friday's test? Chances are, you're giving the wrong pretest.

Throughout the week, use a variety of methods to teach your child how to spell new words. Include both oral and written practice. But since the test will be written, make sure your child can *write* the words correctly.

Here's a trick to use on those few pesky words that boggle your child's mind. Write the word neatly and have your child carefully trace around each word, using straight lines. Lightly color the shape. Then have her study the shape of the word.

66. Make sure your child can read and draw graphs, charts, and maps.

Publishers spend lots of money putting graphs, charts, and maps into textbooks for a reason—they're important. Make certain your child can read and draw them. They often show up on tests.

Graphs, charts, and maps punctuate math, science, and social studies books. Don't overlook them. Often in color, these visual aids bring clarity to otherwise confusing text.

67. Practice answering essay and open-ended questions.

Gone are the days of multiple choice, fill-in-the-bubble sheet standardized tests. Today's exams require students to answer open-ended questions in all content areas, including mathematics, reading, science, and social studies. Writing exams test children's ability to construct various forms of text, such as narrative, expository, persuasive, and even poetry. And some states' exams require children to deliver a speech in front of their classmates. It's no surprise that teachers, in preparing their students for these standardized exams, are developing similar tests for classroom use.

You can practice these kinds of questions with your child by asking him to explain, compare, summarize, or describe. Showing your child how to develop a quick outline or graphic organizer will also help him earn good grades on these exams.

68.

Use mnemonic devices to help your child memorize facts and difficult spelling words.

"Every Good Boy Does Fine" helps the beginning music student remember the lines of the treble clef scale. Mnemonic devices are memory aids, or tricks, that help children remember lists, spellings, and facts. Do you spell your sweet reward that follows supper *d-e-s-e-r-t* or *d-e-s-s-e-r-t?* You'll never forget when you remember there is sand in the desert and strawberry shortcake is a delicious dessert.

Help your child make up her own mnemonic devices when studying for tests, or whenever she needs to remember information. They can be zany or serious. The only trick is finding a trick that works for your child.

When my best friend's wife gave birth to their second daughter, I had difficulty remembering who was the youngest, until I realized, "Kate came late." I haven't mixed up the girls' names since, which is a real feat for me. Your child will remember some mnemonic devices for a lifetime, while others may be forgotten moments after taking the test. But having fun with mnemonic devices will certainly yield higher test grades.

Question: Why is it so hard to remember how to spell *mnemonic?*

69.

Teach your child to write down any questions the teacher asks during lectures.

Wouldn't it be great if teachers gave their students the test questions before they gave the test? Often, they do! Teachers inherently want their students to do well on tests. That's why teachers spend one full class period reviewing before a major exam. During that review, they pose questions to the class. Often, the same or similar questions appear on the test.

By writing down the questions that the teacher asks during the lectures and review, your child will have many exam questions written in her notebook. By studying the questions and their answers, you child will be well prepared for the test.

70. Allow your child to study with friends.

Encourage your child to invite a friend over to do homework or study for a test. Remember, active learning is better than passive learning, especially when followed by a soft drink and a slice of pizza.

Actively studying with a friend will reap big rewards. Talk is a method of communication that kids know well, and when applied to schoolwork, it can be more effective than hours of reading. Just make certain you stay within earshot. As long as the talk if focused on studying, learning is happening, in spite of the giggles and noise.

71. Teach your child to think.

While watching television, take advantage of commercial breaks to ask your child what he thinks will happen next in the show, why he thinks the main character did what she did, and what might be the consequences if the character does what he thinks she will do.

This activity will help your child do better in all subjects in school. Reading teachers ask children to identify main ideas, make inferences, predict outcomes, and draw conclusions. It's easy to see how these same skills are applicable to social studies, science, and mathematics, too. With a little thought, you can raise television viewing from a boob tube activity to a brain-linking, thinking activity.

72. Make your child a better thinker by asking "Why?"

Remember when your child drove you crazy by asking "Why?"Now you can make her a better thinker by asking the same question. "Why is there a stop sign on that corner? Why is it wrong to cheat? Why were racial tensions so high in the 1960s? Why did we fight in Vietnam? Why aren't you allowed to stay out past midnight?"

73.
After asking a question, give your child time to think.

People inherently hate to wait, but children need time to organize their thoughts and retrieve the right words.

Silence is golden, except following a direct question. Then it's perceived as ignorance, inattentiveness, denial, or lingering. It takes longer for children to formulate answers to academic questions than social questions because academic questions require precise vocabulary and specific detail.

Give your child time to think, and never answer for him. If your child cannot answer by the time you silently count to ten slowly, rephrase the question, or give some additional information and ask a new question.

74. Honor your child's opinions.

Provide your child with a safe environment where he can express opinions without fear of reprisal. Encourage him to respectfully express his opinions in school, too.

Do your hackles rise when your child expresses an opinion contrary to yours? "I think it's silly that we go to Grandpop's every Sunday. I'd rather stay home and play with my friends."

Instead of blasting him with a guilt trip, "Don't you love your grandfather enough to visit him once a week?" try acknowledging his feelings, "I understand. Sometimes I'd rather play tennis, but your grandfather looks forward to our visit."

Your child's independent thinking will blossom when he is permitted to express his opinions without retaliation.

75. Encourage your child to make puzzles.

Assembling puzzles develops hand-eye coordination and helps children see spatial relationships and improve problem-solving skills.

Buy age-appropriate puzzles. Toddlers can manipulate large wooden puzzles with five pieces or less. Puzzles with 25 pieces challenge preschoolers, while 100- to 250-piece puzzles keep most elementary school children entertained for an hour or more. For a family activity, serve up a 500- to 1,000-piece challenge, accompanied by a large bowl of hot popcorn.

76. Give your young child many opportunities to practice cutting, coloring, and drawing.

These activities develop hand-eye coordination and fine motor control in preschool children. Buy child-size scissors with rounded tips and teach your child to use them safely. Large, uncluttered coloring books are best for young children. Provide large sheets of paper for drawing. Shapes, in order of difficulty, are circle, cross, rectangle, triangle, diamond.

P.S. Your child's drawings make beautiful gift-wrapping paper.

77.

Hang a U.S. map and world map in your child's bedroom, and keep a globe handy.

Does your child know where Israel and Iran are located? Why was Hawaii so strategically important during World War II? How far is it to Disney World? Which states will we pass through on the way to grandmother's house?

Children need to develop a sense of distance and place. Maps and globes do it best. Use these visual aides and your child will better understand the world around him.

78. Watch the world news on television with your child (local news is mostly fires and murders), and talk about it.

All is seldom quiet on the Eastern front . . . or the Asian front . . . or the European front. World Peace. Global Market. NATO. The United Nations. OPEC. The world really is becoming a smaller place and the happenings in one region definitely affect people in other regions, near and far.

CNN calls it "The World Today"—teachers call it current events. Your child will enjoy participating in classroom, lunchroom, and dinner table discussions when she watches the world news on television regularly.

Television news is presented in short, chopped-up segments, which are sometimes difficult for adults to assimilate, so your child may need help sorting things out. Watch the news together and talk about it. Point out how events taking place on the other side of the globe directly impact our daily lives. To help your child maintain perspective, keep a world map under the couch or on top of the TV set.

79. Use a simple time line to help your child understand historical sequences.

Washington and Lincoln are often studied together because their birthdays fall in February. Does your child realize that they lived one hundred years apart?

80. Review vocabulary words every day.

Teachers assign lists of vocabulary words in all major subjects: language arts, science, social studies, and mathematics. Most likely, your child also needs to study vocabulary for music, foreign language, computers, home economics, physical education, and other minor subjects he studies in school.

Vocabulary words come home on teacher-made lists and are prominently displayed in textbooks in boldfaced, underlined, italicized, or color print. Show me a teacher who doesn't assign vocabulary words to study, and I'll show you a textbook without words.

81. Teach your child to circle key instructions on papers and tests.

Children frequently lose points on tests because they fail to follow written instructions. Although you can't be with your child during exams, you can help her focus on written directions while working together on homework. Teach her to circle key words. (Use pencil if working from a textbook.) Key words might include *describe, choose, circle, compare, contrast, explain, outline, underline, write.* Then, instruct her to do the same on test papers before answering any questions.

82.

Read the questions at the end of each textbook chapter to your child before he reads the chapter.

Many students read textbooks the same way they read novels. They breeze along, paying little attention to key points and important information. A good habit to acquire is reading the review questions before reading the text, even when not required to answer them. This prereading strategy helps the student set a purpose for reading and make predictions, and it prepares him to interact with the text. Becoming an active participant in the reading process enables your child to key into important details and come away with better understanding of the material he has read.

83. Before your child reads a textbook chapter or starts a research project, have her jot down what she already knows about the topic.

Then, on the other side of the page, ask her to list what she wants to find out about the topic. This sets a purpose for the assignment beyond the obvious one.

84.

Practice summarizing a story, textbook chapter, or television program with your child.

Help him identify main ideas and sequence events from beginning, middle, to end.

Summarizing and retelling signals understanding. When your child can summarize a story and put textbook information into his own words, he'll be able to join discussions and answer teachers' questions in class. This skill also prepares students to answer essay questions on exams, which require concise, organized responses.

85. Help your child investigate projects for extra credit.

Many teachers give students opportunities to earn extra credit. Ask your child, or her teacher, if he routinely offers extra-credit assignments.

Extra credit provides an opportunity for a student to bring up her average after bombing a test or forgetting an occasional homework assignment. But it won't rescue the student who never studies or rarely completes homework. The best defense (against low grades) is a good offense. Get your child into the habit of studying for tests and completing homework on schedule. Then she can relax, knowing that extra credit provides the safety in case of an occasional fumble.

86. Help your child use his talents to explore projects from new angles.

Help your child discover and use his talents and special abilities. These can be great resources for both academic and extracurricular activities.

Teachers often give choices for how a project may be done. Help your child choose a method most suited to his talents. Rather than writing a report, suggest that your child artist paint a picture or your gregarious actor videotape himself role-playing the scene. Most likely, the teacher will enjoy the change of pace as much as your child will.

87.

Ask your child to teach you something she learned in school today.

People remember 10 percent of what they read, 20 percent of what they hear, 30 percent of what they see, 50 percent of what they see and hear, 70 percent of what they say as they talk aloud, and 90 percent of what they say as they perform a task. Teaching is talking and performing. When your child teaches you a concept introduced in school, she has mastered it.

88. Teach your child how and when to use calculators, word processors, and electronic dictionaries.

When your child uses modern technology, she is not cheating. Would you really want your secretary to use a manual typewriter or your accountant to figure your income tax returns using a #2 pencil and a big eraser?

Children need to learn basic math calculations, writing skills, and how to use reference materials. You won't get any argument on that one from me. But humans are superior to animals because they have the ability to transfer knowledge from one being to the next and from one generation to the next. In the twenty-first century, technology is knowledge. Even a one-room schoolhouse will be linked to the world through the Internet. So, teach your child how to use technology to keep ahead in school and expand horizons.

Question: What do you do when the batteries go dead?
Answer: Buy new batteries.

89.

Teach your child how to use your local library, including electronic search devices, interlibrary loan systems, CD-ROM database programs, and Internet search services.

Does your child know that if your library doesn't own a copy of the book he's searching for, chances are the librarian can obtain it from another source in about a week? That's called interlibrary loan. And if he needs an article from a magazine that's not in stock, your librarian might have it faxed within an hour? Or it might be available on a CD-ROM database?

Students in junior and senior high school require more sophisticated research tools, available at local, county, or metropolitan libraries. But your child must learn how to use them. It's a good idea to spend an afternoon leisurely learning what's available and how to use it, rather than waiting until deadline pressures burden the task.

90. Encourage your child to learn how to touch-type.

Computers are everywhere in schools today. If you own a home computer, invest in a typing tutor program.

It's far easier to learn a task correctly the first time than to unlearn bad habits later. Preschoolers today are as familiar with a computer mouse as they are with Mickey Mouse. And although preschoolers are not developmentally ready to learn touch-typing skills, children should begin practicing proper techniques as soon as possible. About fourth or fifth grade is a good time to start. Practicing fifteen minutes a day will increase your child's keyboarding proficiency, enabling him to breeze through writing assignments.

91.

Teach your child to use a basic word-processing program.

Computers are here to stay. By the time your child is in fourth grade, he should know how to use a basic word-processing program, including cut, paste, spellcheck, and thesaurus features.

You bought that home computer to help your child do better in school, but all he does is play games and surf the Internet. Finally, here's a legitimate use for your PC that really nets results.

The advantages of word processing are the same for children as for adults. Writing tasks are completed faster, editing is

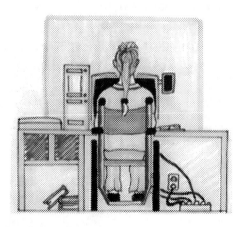

easier, revising is a snap, and the final copy is neat, clean, and legible. But in order for word processing to be a real boon, your child must become independent at the keyboard. He needs to be able to start up the CPU, boot the program, begin on a blank screen, and save his work. Children learn quickly and breeze through these basic lessons. The only thing that seems to take as long for youngsters to learn as adults is saving their work every ten minutes or at the end of every paragraph.

Once your child can cut, paste, and spellcheck with the best of them, word processing will be a godsend to his homework routine.

92. Supervise computer activities.

It sounds great when children say they're working on the computer, but if all they're doing is killing fourteen million monsters and splattering their guts all over the space station, it's not of any educational value.

No one can refute that the home computer is the most powerful educational tool ever conceived. But it can also be the most powerful homework-interrupting device ever invented (after television). Participate with your child in computer games, supervise on-line activities, and teach how to use educational software. Since most CD-ROM titles are purchased by parents, you *do* have control over computer activities.

For expert advice on purchasing software, consult a popular computer magazine. September back-to-school issues and December holiday issues usually critique entertainment and educational software.

93.

Introduce yourself to the school bus driver.

Children may spend between twenty minutes and two hours riding a school bus every day. If your child rides the bus to school, get to know the driver. Make it a point to be at the bus stop occasionally to wave hello and remind the driver that you care. Your child's life is in her hands. Check that the kids are obeying bus safety rules, which allow the driver to focus her attention on the road. Although learning takes place beyond the bus stop, a pleasant, comfortable, and safe trip will deposit your child at school with a positive attitude, ready to learn.

94. Set up a conference to meet with your child's teacher(s) two weeks after school begins or two weeks after moving to a new school district.

This is what I call an "I'd like to get to know you" meeting. (Attending Back-to-School Night doesn't count for this one.) Taking the initiative to meet your child's teacher early in the school year lays the groundwork for a successful parent-teacher partnership. This is the perfect time for you to get to know the teacher and for her to get to know both you and your child.

During this brief conference (usually about twenty minutes), talk about your child's strengths and weaknesses. Tell the teacher which subject is most difficult for your child and discuss any health needs that may affect learning or school attendance. Clue her in on what works and doesn't work for your child. Don't leave your child's education to chance. Months may pass before the teacher figures it all out for herself. Before leaving, decide when and where to call each other (at night at home or at a specific time in school) and exchange phone numbers.

95. Join the PTA and attend meetings regularly.

The National PTA does more than sponsor bake sales. This 6.5-million-member organization, with more than 26,000 local units, acts as a legislative watchdog and much more. National PTA observances include:

- America Goes Back to School Week (August)
- American Education Week (November)
- World AIDS Day (December)
- Earth Week (April)
- Teacher Appreciation Week (May)

If your school is not affiliated with the National PTA, chances are it has an established PTO or other parent-teacher group that works closely with parents, teachers, administrators, community leaders, and businesses to benefit children in your school. Get to know the other parents who make a difference in your child's school. Join up, and you will make a difference too.

96. Keep lines of communication open with your child's teacher.

I often need to reach parents during the day, but with mom and dad both working, I hesitate to place calls at the work site, unless prior permission has been given. Exchange phone numbers and times to call.

Inform your child's teacher if you are available to receive phone calls during the day, or if you prefer he leave a message on your answering machine, send a note home with your child, or e-mail you. Failure to communicate remains a major complaint of both parents and teachers. Avoid this pitfall by clearly communicating how to get in touch. A brief phone call or quick note provides a vital link to your child's academic success. Use them often.

97. Provide the teacher with ten stamped, self-addressed postcards to promote regular communication.

The number one complaint of both parents and teachers is lack of communication. This tip provides a simple solution. Ask the teacher to to drop you a note whenever she feels it necessary.

Because postcards are small, your child's teacher can quickly write one or two lines without feeling obligated to send a lengthy letter. Comments like "Failed to turn in two math assignments this week" or "Spelling is much improved" are all it takes to keep lines of communication open. Your child's teacher will also appreciate that the cards are preaddressed, so all he need do is drop them in the school's outgoing mailbox.

Here's a word of precaution. Some savvy adolescents intercept the mail. If you think this may be a problem, consider addressing the postcards to your place of business.

98.

Volunteer to help with one classroom activity or to be a guest reader in your child's class.

It's a jungle in there! Some teachers openly ask for parent volunteers, others don't. But if you've ever hosted a child's birthday party with a dozen small guests running pell-mell through your house, you'll appreciate why a teacher welcomes a second set of hands. Teachers often ask for help during field trips and holiday parties, but there are at least 175 other days when your help may be appreciated. If you're really brave, volunteer to chaperone a field trip or school dance.

Being a guest reader is rewarding to both you and the children. Choose a book with a tie-in to your work or hobby (ask the teacher's assistance if needed). After reading the book, talk about your own experiences as they relate to the book. Then be prepared to answer questions about a subject you already know well. It really is fun.

Volunteering also allows you to meet the other children. That way, when your child talks about her friends, you can say, "Oh, yeah, I know who Julieanne is. I met her the day I volunteered in your classroom."

99.

Be your child's Show 'n Tell.

What better way is there to show your child that school is important? What better way is there for your child to show how proud she is of Mom or Dad? What better way is there for your child's teacher to get to know you? What better way is there for you to get to meet your child's schoolmates?

100.

Talk to the teacher if your child has special needs.

Teachers are not psychics. If your child wears glasses, tell her teacher. You'd be surprised how long glasses remain buried in a child's desk before an unsuspecting teacher discovers them.

Some children resist wearing glasses, especially when they need them only for reading. Tell the teacher if your child should be wearing glasses for reading up close or copying from the chalkboard. If you are one of those parents plagued by frequently lost eyeglasses, consider buying two pairs if you can afford them. Instruct your child to leave one pair in school, and keep the other at home.

101. If you suspect your child has a learning disability, request a multidisciplinary team evaluation through your local school.

Special education rules and regulations are complex, and whole books have been written to explain them. But be aware that your child has the right to an evaluation (free of charge) to determine if a learning disability exists.

Most people are familiar with dyslexia, a disability associated with learning to read, but a child may have a learning disability in writing, mathematics, and/or language, also. Your child's teacher is a good first resource. In fact, classroom teachers are often the first to suspect a child has a learning disability. So ask your child's teacher. If she agrees, ask her to initiate the referral. If not, request a conference with a member of your school's multidisciplinary team. (Every school has one, or access to one.)

Here's an important reminder. Identifying that a child has a learning disability won't make her difficulties go away, but it will give you the tools to help her succeed in school.

102.

Tell the school about family crises.

Children behave differently under stress. Some act out, while others withdraw into themselves. Alerting the teacher about a family crisis—the death of a grandparent, the loss of a pet, or a serious family illness—will enable her to manage your child's emotional needs more appropriately. All it takes is a two-minute phone call or short note.

Teachers appreciate knowing when unfortunate situations may affect their students. It's a time when many find a few extra minutes to show a child they care.

103. Send your child's teacher a birthday card.

Teachers are generous people. Throughout the school year, they spend countless hours decorating classrooms, arranging special events, and volunteering their time to help others— not to mention digging into their own pockets to supplement school supplies and activities.

Sending a birthday greeting shows that you and your child appreciate the little things she does to make school enjoyable. If you don't know your teacher's birthday, simply ask her at Back-to-School Night or at an early conference. Or, you may ask the principal's secretary. Just tell her you want to send the teacher a birthday card and she'll be happy to help you.

104.

Don't wait until June to send your child's teacher a thank-you card.

Jot a note telling her how much your child enjoyed the science project or book she read in class. Let her know what's working with your child.

Teachers need positive feedback as much as their students do. Telling the teacher what methods are working with your child assures her that she's in the right ballpark. Teachers try new techniques all the time and judge whether they scored a hit or a foul ball by students' reactions, test scores, and parent feedback. But the latter is rare. So the next time your child bursts through the front door shouting, "Guess what we did in school today!" be sure to tell the teacher she hit a home run.

105.

Make a pact with your child's teacher that states, "If you don't believe everything my child says about me, I won't believe everything he says about you."

Children exaggerate. They don't necessarily lie, but their perceptions may be skewed. Whether your child describes his teacher as the Wicked Witch of the West or Mary Poppins, keep in mind that all may not be as he perceives.

106. If you disagree with your child's teacher, talk with her privately.

Sometimes it happens. Your child's teacher does something that curls the hairs on the back of your neck. Maybe she punishes the whole class when only a few were misbehaving. Or you're fed up with the "busywork" she assigns every night. Finally, you've HAD IT UP TO HERE!

You say to your child, "That stupid Mrs. So-and-So! Who does she think she is? I know drill sergeants who would make better teachers than that #*&@!"

Then you talk with the teacher. You hear her side of the story. You negotiate. You understand . . . well, you tolerate. Things aren't quite as they had seemed. You move on. But where is your child?

The teacher gives another assignment. Your child thinks, "That stupid Mrs. So-and-So! Who does she think she is? If she wants to learn about tree frogs, she can look them up herself. I ain't doing no #*&@! report!"

Put your anger on hold; don't put down the teacher in front of your child.

107.

Always be your child's advocate but never become the teacher's adversary.

If you feel your child has been wronged, defend her. Call the teacher, have a conference, work things out the best you can, but don't make the teacher the enemy. When parents and teachers are openly hostile toward each other, the child almost always becomes the loser.

108. Before you attend a parent-teacher conference, ask your child, "What's the hardest thing about school?"

Your child's answer might be something expected, like reading, or it might be a real shocker, like the playground. Whatever his response, talk with him about it and then discuss it with his teacher.

109. Take notes during parent-teacher conferences.

It's easy to forget details, especially if your child has several teachers. Taking notes shows teachers that you're serious about working with them. When you get home, review your notes. If you discover something isn't clear, call the teacher for further explanation. Then review the highlights of the conference with your child. Help her understand that you and her teacher will be working together to help her succeed in school.

110. During Back-to-School night, be sure to meet your child's other teachers: art, music, shop, library, gym.

Physical education and creative arts teachers often teach every student in the building. Think about it. If a teacher teaches six hundred children, what will make your child stand out among the crowd? Help your child succeed in these classes by introducing yourself and letting these specialists know that you're on their team. Volunteering to help during one class period will certainly put you, and your child, ahead of the pack. (You may also learn that teaching art class is more than just making Valentine cards.)

111. If your child constantly complains about school, it's time to take action.

Your child will spend at least thirteen years in school. If she always complains about school or seems angry with her teacher, something is wrong.

School should be a rewarding, enjoyable place where your child stretches her mind and develops lasting friendships. Although school might not top your child's favorite places list, it shouldn't conjure up nightmares, either.

Talk with your child. Find out what's bugging her. Getting specific details (M. J. makes rude comments to me), rather than vague descriptions (M. J. is such a nerd), will enable you to take action, either by talking with your child or with her teacher or counselor.

112.

When the teacher requests a conference because your child is misbehaving, consider having your child attend the meeting.

Very young children may be unaware that their behavior is annoying the teacher. At home, youngsters blurt out questions, run around the living room at will, and go to the bathroom when nature calls. Sometimes, just realizing that the teacher is serious about changing the behavior is all the child needs to begin acting more appropriately.

Bringing an older youngster to a disciplinary meeting may be crucial, especially when more than one teacher is involved.

At this meeting, with teachers, parent, and youngster present, you can lay down the ground rules, establish consequences, and develop a communication system so that everyone knows the expectations, leaving little room for the youngster to out-maneuver anybody.

Tempers can fly in disciplinary meetings. Try these strategies to keep the meeting proactive:

- Spend 20 percent of the time talking about the problem and 80 percent of the time discussing solutions.
- Don't belittle your child in front of his teacher.
- Don't blame the teacher.
- Establish a means of communicating *daily* with the teacher.
- Select a date for a follow-up meeting.

113.
If your child is uncomfortable changing for gym, talk with the gym teacher, guidance counselor, or school nurse.

Talk with your child to find out exactly what's bothering him. Perhaps you can make arrangements for your child to change in the nurse's office, or to wear sweats instead of shorts.

For some youngsters, changing in front of peers is a big deal. Don't allow your child to fail gym because he's embarrassed. Instead, make arrangements to ensure participation, which is what really counts.

114. If your child says that school is boring, find out why.

If your school's curriculum is not challenging your child, he should be getting very high grades without much effort. If so, request a conference immediately. More likely, your child is tuning out and copping out. Request a conference immediately.

115. Make certain your child gets a good night's sleep.

Depending on your child's age, he needs between eight and ten hours sleep each night. Establish a reasonable bedtime and stick to it. Your child must be alert to succeed in school. Imagine a young person struggling to absorb a day's worth of education when he can't keep his eyes open and his head up off the desk.

You may think your child is getting proper rest, but take a close look at your bedtime routine. How long does it take from the time he marches up the stairs until he closes his eyes? Getting washed, brushing teeth, and reading a bedtime story may take forty minutes or longer.

Not everyone is a morning person, but your child should wake up refreshed. If he spends most of the morning dragging around the house, chances are, he's not getting enough sleep.

116. Allow enough time in the mornings.

Don't you just hate flying out the front door in the morning with one shoe off and a bagel jammed in your mouth? So do kids. Your child should wake up early enough to wash, dress, eat, and leave home in a relaxed mood.

117.
Make sure your child eats a good breakfast each morning.

Children cannot satisfy intellectual needs if their physical needs haven't been met. Or, to put it more simply—kids can't learn with their stomachs growling.

118. Kiss or hug your child each morning.

Send your child off to school with a warm heart.
Do children with warm hearts really do better in school?
You bet!

119. Make sure your child is ready on gym days.

Know which days your child has gym and see to it that she has a proper change of clothing or sneakers if they are required at her grade level.

Kids fail gym for three reasons:

1. They are not prepared.
2. They do not participate.
3. They misbehave.

Where I live, students must take, and pass, four years of physical education to receive their high school diplomas. Students often fail high school gym because they developed poor habits in elementary and junior high school. Your child need not be a star athlete, but she'll avoid many hassles by developing good habits in the earlier grades.

120.

Set up a special area for school items near the front door.

Your child should put everything he needs for the next day on the table: book bag, lunch money, finished science project, musical instrument. (It's a good place to keep the car keys, too.) This reduces morning frenzies over misplaced articles and in-school heart failure over forgotten supplies.

121.

Set up an emergency plan for forgotten items.

When adults forget, we joke about having Alzheimer's Disease, but when kids forget, we yell at them. When your child occasionally forgets something, resolve the problem without getting angry.

It's bound to happen. Your child skips off to school eager to learn but then realizes he has forgotten something. It might be a textbook, a homework paper, gym clothes, lunch money, or his musical instrument. His day will be a disaster unless you come to the rescue. You can be a real hero by planning ahead.

Give him permission to call you (most schools permit students to use the pay phone). Make certain he knows where to reach you and has sufficient change to make the call. Find out what time of the day he needs the forgotten item. With a little luck, you'll be able to deliver the goods in the nick of time.

122.

Make certain your child practices good hygiene habits.

Kids are vicious when it comes to B.O., bad breath, and stinky feet. Being the brunt of other kids' teasing will make school a miserable place for your child. Remind her to brush her teeth, wash her hair, and change her socks. If acne strikes, take your child to a dermatologist if financially it's feasible. Help your child prevent being ridiculed by others.

123. Buy clothing that helps your child fit in.

Clothes don't make the person, but children really do need to fit in. You don't have to outfit your child with $150 sneakers and designer jeans, but don't make him look like something out of a Norman Rockwell painting, either.

Fads come and fads go. And, for the most part, their comings and goings are rather fun to watch. Remember bell-bottom trousers and platform shoes? How about untied sneakers that flopped when you walked? And blue jeans that dropped to the floor if you didn't amble like a bowlegged cowboy?

As a parent, you may need to choose your fashion battles cautiously. Most public schools seem to allow tattoos and body piercing (including nose and tongue) but still ban midriff blouses, bare feet, and T-shirts advertising beer, alcohol, tobacco, drugs, firearms, and satanism. Parents are left with the unenviable task of balancing fashions that allow their child to fit in, without freaking themselves out.

124.
Don't allow your child to be absent or late to school unless there's a medical reason.

To succeed in school, your child must be in school. Chicken pox or a bout with the flu may keep your child homebound for a week or two. That doesn't leave much time for those "I don't feel like going to school today" vacations.

Every household faces an occasional panic-filled morning when the alarm clock fails or the car battery dies. Nobody will hassle your child about that. But teachers are incensed when children are frequently late to school. Here's why:

- After arriving late, the child spends additional time in the office explaining his tardiness.
- The child misses first-period instruction (in elementary school, this means reading or math).
- The child is disciplined first thing in the morning, putting him in a bad mood, which interferes with learning the rest of the day.
- Children who don't get enough sleep at night are still tired after arriving late to school.
- Children who oversleep usually don't eat breakfast.
- Children are sometimes late because they are getting into mischief on the way to school.

125.

Schedule family vacations to coincide with school holidays.

I'm the last person to argue the educational value of travel. But think about it. In many states, school is in session about 180 days a year. That leaves 185 days to travel without pulling your child out of school.

Teachers spend hundreds of hours planning lessons, grading papers, and ensuring curriculum requirements are delivered according to time lines established by your local board of education. It's only human to become annoyed when these efforts are ignored by parents who remove their children midstream for a family vacation. Compounding their aggravation is that parents ask teachers to perform additional tasks of preparing assignments in advance, providing makeup exams (which often means writing a new test), and tutoring their child when he returns to catch him up with the rest of the class.

Although your child will certainly enjoy his vacation, he too will suffer frustration and anxiety, trying to catch up. It takes some children several weeks to recover from a seven-day absence. Don't purposefully put your child at a disadvantage.

126. Teach your child to be a responsible person.

Irresponsible children don't do their assigned chores, frequently leave needed books in school, and announce at bedtime that they forgot to study for a test. But children don't develop skills and attitudes that lead to responsible behavior by osmosis. They must be taught.

You can teach your child how to do chores by demonstrating the task step-by-step. Never redo the job, even if it's not perfect. This sends a message that her work isn't good enough.

You can also model how your child can fulfill school responsibilities. Teach her to set up a daily schedule, to pack her bookbag by checking her homework assignment book, and to develop a study schedule for tests and long-term reports.

Teaching your child self-discipline, dependability, and accountability will benefit her now and will pay off later in high school, in college, and on the job.

127. Schedule a vision exam if your child is struggling with reading.

Your child should be able to read her textbooks without too much trouble. If she is getting stuck on every fourth word, or if she can't answer simple factual questions after reading a short passage, she might have a learning disability. Or, she may have a vision problem.

It is estimated that 11 percent of school-aged children have a learning disability. Sometimes called the "hidden handicap," learning disabilities occur in all children, regardless of race, gender, ethnic origin, or economic status.

But other factors also interfere with reading. Don't overlook the obvious—poor visual acuity (nearsightedness and farsightedness). Ocular muscle imbalance can also cause words to jump around the printed page. A thorough vision exam is always a good place to start when your child is having difficulty learning to read.

128. Make sure your child has all required immunizations and booster shots.

Help your child stay healthy and avoid being absent from school. More importantly, help prevent your child from becoming deathly ill. While some assert that childhood diseases are mere nuisances, the truth is, they can be deadly.

When ninety-six students at Rutgers University in New Jersey came down with measles in 1994, the N.J. Department of Health declared a state of emergency, ordering vaccinations for nearly 29,000 people on campus. At a cost of over $500,000, saving even one life was well worth the price.

Of course, it'll cost you far less to protect your child from disease. See your pediatrician or call the Vaccines for Children coordinator in your state. For additional information, call the Centers for Disease Control and Prevention at either of these toll-free numbers.

1-800-CDC-SHOT: for information about vaccines, the immunization schedule, and publications on vaccine-preventable diseases

1-800-232-2522: to locate immunization clinics near you

129. Recognize the signs of a hearing loss.

Middle ear infections, common in young children, sometimes produce temporary or permanent hearing loss, which may cause delays in speech and language development and interfere with learning phonics. Keep a close check on this through your pediatrician.

Parents need to be aware of signs that may indicate a hearing loss. While no one of the following signs positively indicates hearing loss, if your child exhibits one or more, seek professional help:

1. Doesn't hear you call from another room.
2. Strains to watch a speaker or claims to hear better when watching the speaker's face.
3. Fails to pay attention when spoken to.
4. Gives the wrong answer to simple questions.
5. Doesn't hear TV or music at the same loudness level as everyone else.
6. Frequently asks you to repeat words or sentences.
7. Has frequent colds, running ears, upper respiratory infections, or allergies.
8. Doesn't have normal voice quality.

9. Doesn't have normal verbal language development (vocabulary, speech sounds, sentence structure).
10. Functions below potential in school.

130. Discuss with your child the difference between good touching and bad touching.

Good touching feels like a warm fuzzy; bad touching gives you the shivers. Your child should feel safe in knowing that he can always tell you if he ever feels the shivers.

Children cannot learn in school when their minds are preoccupied by terrible thoughts. Abused children often feel guilt and responsibility and assume they are to blame for what happened. In most cases, children are sexually abused by people they know or people who know their families. That's why it's so difficult for them to confide in others.

Talk with your child matter-of-factly about bad touching. Build a strong, loving relationship that guarantees you will never criticize or blame your child. Secure your child's trust, so he informs you before a bad situation turns into a nightmare.

Childhood is the most basic human right of children.
—David Elkind

131. Know the warning signs of alcohol and drug abuse.

Don't ever think it can't happen to your child, or that your child is too young. Children frequently experiment with alcohol and drugs during elementary school years and can become easily addicted at a young age. Talk with your child or seek professional advice if you notice any of these warning signs.

- *Physical:* excessive coughing, red and dull eyes
- *Emotional:* sudden mood changes, low self-esteem, depression
- *Family:* starting arguments or breaking rules, withdrawing from the family
- *School:* drop in grades, many absences
- *Social:* scrapes with the law, a new group of friends, changes in dressing and music

132.

Teach your child the golden rule: "Treat others the way you want to be treated."

Helping your child learn to cooperate and get along with others will enable her to succeed, not only in school, but in everything she does. So, how do you teach your child to show respect for others? By living a good example.

Begin by treating your child with respect. Don't ridicule her in front of friends or adults. Say please and thank you to your child. Respect her right to express opinions, even when different from yours. Then, teach your child to be tolerant of others. Help her understand that legitimate rules are made to protect the welfare of everyone. ("What would school be like if everyone came late to class?") If you observe your child acting unkindly toward someone, talk with her privately about it. Ask how she would feel if she were treated that way.

School is more rewarding for children who live the golden rule. In fact, life is more rewarding for everyone who lives the golden rule.

133. Know your child's friends.

Meet them. Invite them over to your house for popcorn. If you don't approve of your child's friends, help her choose new ones. (Unless she is a teenager, in which case you should talk with her about your concerns.)

Hanging out with the wrong crowd in school spells academic disaster. Whether an eight-year-old befriends the class clown or a teenager hangs with the deadheads, one thing is certain—school performance will take a nosedive.

Remind your child what a good friend is, and that friendships should be mutually satisfying. Encourage her to widen her circle of friends to avoid getting locked into cliques. If your child has a "best friend" whom you haven't met, it's time to roll out the red carpet and invite her or him over for a visit.

134. Teach your child that he is responsible for his own behavior.

If your child gets into trouble with another child, talk with him about ways of ignoring or avoiding the other child. You can ask the teacher to change his seat, but usually this doesn't completely solve the problem.

"He started it . . . She pushed me first . . . It wasn't my fault . . . She called my mother a witch."

Kids will be kids. But when your child continually has difficulty getting along with another, it's time for action. The best person to take charge of your child's behavior is your child. Talk with him. Suggest ways for him to avoid the other child in the classroom, on the playground, after school, or wherever potential trouble lurks. If you know the other child's parents, you may consider talking with them about the situation. If it's serious, by all means tell the teacher or guidance counselor. But expect your child to control his own behavior. Children can squelch many conflicts by learning to ignore verbal attacks. It's easy—just say nothing or walk away.

135.

Make good manners standard operating procedure in your home.

Always say *please, thank you,* and *excuse me.* Your child will mimic your good manners and use them frequently in school.

Courtesy is contagious. A cheery "thanks for the ride" brings a warm "you're welcome" from the bus driver. An apologetic "excuse me for bumping into you" brings an accepting "that's okay" from a classmate. Teachers and other adults notice well-mannered children. When children are noticed in a kind way, smiles and compliments brighten their day.

136.

Teach your child how to accept a compliment, especially from peers.

For some children, compliments are easier to give than to receive. Consequently, children do strange things when given compliments by their peers. Sometimes they say nothing and walk away. Sometimes they negate the compliment with modesty, "It was just dumb luck." And sometimes they hit or inappropriately touch the other person. Guys often punch other guys in the arm and girls push other girls while saying something like, "Oh, get out of here."

Teach your child to accept a compliment by saying "Thank you." It's quick and painless, and provides the giver of the compliment with positive reinforcement.

137. Believe your child when she reports a problem or an incident that occurred in school.

To build trust, it's important that you believe your child, even if you're not quite sure of the circumstances. If the situation directly affects your child, ask permission to discuss it with her teacher. This builds trust. It's important that your child can talk with you confidentially, without fear that you will always inform the authorities. (Of course, sometimes you will have no choice, depending on the nature or severity of the situation.)

138.

Teach your child the difference between tattling and appropriately informing an adult about a dangerous situation.

A good rule of thumb for your child to follow is to tell a teacher whenever he thinks somebody might get hurt or might hurt somebody else.

"Tattletale. Tattletale. Stick you head in a garbage pail."

How many times has your child been told not to tattle? Children often tattle to get others in trouble or to make themselves look good. But your child should inform a teacher or other adult whenever he senses danger. For instance:

- when a three-year-old neighbor is playing in the street
- when a child bullies or threatens another
- when a fistfight breaks out
- when someone flaunts a weapon

139. Teach your child to embrace diversity.

Don't allow racial slurs, jokes about people with disabilities or rude, sexist remarks to be tolerated in your home. Remember, what is practiced at home is shared in school.

140. Never give your child permission to hit another person.

If necessary, teach your child to protect himself from bodily harm, but not to fight. Talk with him about ways to resolve conflicts. He can avoid bullies by finding a safe route to and from school and by surrounding himself with friends in the cafeteria and locker room.

Many schools have peer mediation programs that train students how to resolve conflicts. Your child should ask his teacher or counselor to arrange peer mediation when he is having continual conflict with a particular classmate.

Remind your child that fighting, hitting, and bullying are never acceptable ways of settling conflicts. If he complains of being a wimp, remind him that assault and battery are illegal.

141.
Take action if your child is being teased, verbally abused, or purposefully left out of activities.

Sticks and stones may break my bones but names hurt deep down inside me. When your child is being teased, verbally abused, or purposefully left out of activities, it's a very big and very real problem. Chances are it won't go away by itself. You'll need to take action.

Talk with your child. Find out if he is being teased by one child or many. Acknowledge his feelings. Show that you understand how much it hurts. Encourage your child to join clubs, activities, or organizations where he can find new friends with similar interests. If teasing occurs on the playground, call the parent of a friendly classmate. Make arrangements for the two children to meet and play together. Don't hesitate to call the teacher or principal if teasing persists. Teasing can often be curtailed under a teacher's watchful eye.

> Everything is funny as long as it is happening to somebody else.
> —Will Rogers

142. Under no circumstances allow your child to be bullied.

Bullying is harassment. Bullying takes the form of persistent verbal teasing and ridicule, or physical abuse. About one in five children has been the victim of bullying. Bullying can leave deep emotional scars for life. Bullying is not "Kids will be kids." Bullying is serious and must never be tolerated.

Here are some warning signs:

- avoiding school
- drop in grades
- requests for extra money or school supplies
- torn clothing
- bruises

Bullying can occur anywhere, but prime locations include on the way to and from school, on the bus, on the playground, in the cafeteria, and in the locker room. Suggest that your child surround herself with friends and try to avoid the bully in these locations. When confronted, your child should try to control her temper (say nothing) and avoid crying. The best defense is to smile, walk away, and then tell an adult.

Most schools have strict rules about bullying. Bullying is harassment and harassment is illegal. Your child has the right to learn in a safe environment. Above all, remember that it's the bully who has the problem. Never blame your child for being a victim.

143. Give praise and reward effort and improvement for social growth on report cards.

Parents frequently reward academic success, but what about social growth? The other side of the report card addresses how well your child gets along with others, pays attention in class, follows directions, completes tasks on time, respects the rights and feelings of others, shares, and cooperates. Developing good social skills will benefit your child throughout her lifetime. So, the next time your child brings home her report card, make a big fuss over improvement shown on the other side of the report card, too.

144. Give your child unconditional love.

Of course you love your child, but sometimes parents unintentionally send a wrong message. "You brought home a great report card. I love you." Does this mean you love your child because she brought home a good report card? Would you ever say, "You failed science. I love you"? Or, "If you loved me you'd do better in school."

Try this, instead. "You brought home a great report card. You make me proud," or "I'm disappointed. You failed science. We'll need to work together to improve your grade."

145. Don't compare your child to others.

Avoid comments like "Juan does so much better in school than you" or "Why can't you make me proud like Alaina makes her mother proud?"

Comparing your child to another may cause your child to become angry with you and resent the other youngster. It matters little whether your child does better than another. What matters is that he is doing the best he can.

146. Don't allow your child to develop a self-defeating attitude.

Never allow your child to say "I can't." Instead, teach her to say "I don't understand this" or "I find this difficult."

Don't allow a self-defeating attitude to inhibit your child's learning. Saying "I can't" initiates a nuclear meltdown of the mind. Urge your child to accept that learning may sometimes be difficult, but not impossible. Assure her that—together—you will triumph.

> No one knows what he can do till he tries.
> —Publilius Syrus (c. 43 B.C.)

147. Reward effort, not grades.

Celebrate your child's best effort, regardless of the grade on top of the test paper. Hugs are the best rewards.

Not all students earn A's all the time. And some students, try as they might, hardly ever earn A's.

Did your child spend hours studying mathematical equations, only to earn a C on the final exam? Did she practice spelling words with you in the car, at the kitchen table, before bedtime, all week long, just to score 85 on Friday's test? Show her how proud you are of her effort.

148.

When your child brings home her report card, resist the urge to point out her lowest grade.

Your child earns two A's, three B's, and one C. So which grade becomes the focus of the report card? In most cases, the lowest one. Show your child how proud you are of her accomplishments and don't ruin the moment by asking "but why didn't you do better here?"

Wait a week, and then announce that you will work with her to improve her lowest grade. She'll be more willing to accept the help when it's offered as a partnership agreement, rather than as punishment.

149. Develop an action plan to combat poor grades.

Rather than punishing your child when she shows you a poor test paper or report card grade, develop an action plan to help her do better next time.

1. *Determine the cause.* Was it lack of preparation, inability to grasp the concepts, poor test-taking skills, or failure to know that the test was scheduled?

2. *Develop a plan.* Call the teacher. Ask her opinion about what caused the low grade. Tell her that you're committed to helping your child improve. Schedule fifteen to thirty minutes each night for studying with your child. Mark the next test date on your calendar. Restrict TV or set a curfew if needed.

3. *Work hard.* Make studying a team effort, rather than a child's punishment. Prove that you're serious about wanting better grades by working with your child nightly. Read or review the textbook or do practice problems, even when homework isn't assigned. Studying each night will yield big rewards, compared to cramming the night before the test.

4. *Celebrate the victory.* When your child improves her grade, even slightly, celebrate the victory. Treat her to the zoo or to the movies. Show her you are proud of her accomplishment.

150. Teach your child to keep an open mind.

Sir James Dewar once said, "Minds are like parachutes. They only function when they are open." Keep an open mind when talking with your child and encourage her to keep an open mind about things she is learning in school.

Have you already answered "No" before your child finishes asking "May I go . . . ?" Does your child remark "This is so stupid" before her teacher finishes giving the assignment?

Students need to understand why teachers give certain assignments. (They're not all busywork.) Help your child see the proverbial forest that's formed by all those trees. Did the teacher assign that research report on school violence just so she has a grade for the report card? Or does she have broader reasons in mind?

151. Don't restrict your child's enthusiasm.

I remember getting angry when my son balked about leaving a hands-on science museum after spending five hours turning dials, pushing buttons, and manipulating interactives. I reassessed the situation, stayed with him, and let the management throw us out two hours later when they locked the doors.

Interactive museums allow children to try on many different hats. With unrestricted enthusiasm, you never know which hat your child will find fits him perfectly.

152. Don't stifle your child's imagination.

Must hearts always be red and shamrocks green? Think how boring life would be without purple dinosaurs and pointy-eared Vulcans.

Imagine the night sky, a boundless void of black nothingness. Then, somewhere on earth, a child imagines, "What if . . . witches were beautiful?" And a speck of light dots the blackness. Then, another child imagines, "What if . . . roses were blue?" And another smidgen joins the first. Then ten more children imagine and ten more points of light twinkle in the night sky. Then ten times ten children imagine. Soon the black nothingness is aglow with billions of imaginations, all glowing and filling the universe with endless possibilities . . . until an adult enters the children's world.

"A beautiful witch? Don't be absurd. Witches are ugly." And a twinkling light fades. Then another grown-up stifles a child's dream, "Roses can't be blue." Another star disappears. And soon, adults all over the world are telling children that their imaginations cannot come true. And the lights die, and the night sky reverts to a boundless void of black nothingness.

Don't stifle your child's imagination. Let her light up the night sky.

153.

Encourage your child to ask questions.

Prove to your child that there is no such thing as a stupid question by always accepting her question and giving a legitimate answer. If she feels comfortable asking you today if Hitler really was a bad person, then most likely she will be comfortable asking you tomorrow about safe sex.

154.
Slip a funny greeting card or an "I love you" note in your child's lunch bag to brighten his day.

Hallmark earns millions of dollars each year selling greeting cards. Actually, they don't sell cards; they sell the opportunity for people to make loved ones feel good.

To succeed in school, children must feel good about being in school. A simple greeting card, whether store-bought or hand-scribbled, will surely brighten your child's day.

155.

Brighten your child's day with a lunch-time surprise.

Everyone loves a surprise. But finding candy corn in your lunch bag in October isn't much of a shock. Flabbergast your child with a slice of pumpkin pie in September, a dyed hard-boiled egg in November, a Trick-or-Treat bag of goodies in January, or Irish potatoes in May. Discover other ways to break lunch bag boredom: holiday napkins, colored plastic wrap, chicken nuggets, popcorn, a gingerbread man.

156.

Project a positive attitude about your own learning.

Telling your child that you always hated math when you were in school sends the message that it's okay for her to hate it, too.

Be careful not to give your child an excuse to do poorly in school. Kids often claim to hate a particular subject or teacher, when, in fact, they find the subject matter difficult or the teacher demanding.

Help your child understand the real problem and work toward a solution. Try saying, "I know math is difficult for you. Let's sit down together and I'll help you with your homework."

157.
Don't label—or let others label—your child as *lazy, immature,* or *bad.*

Labels like these give an excuse, rather than identify a problem. Adjectives such as *lazy, immature,* and *bad* not only place the blame for failure on the child, but also suggest there's no way to remedy the situation. What do you do with an immature child—put him in the back of the classroom until he matures?

When a teacher labels your child, ask what specific behaviors led to that description. Is a child "lazy" because he doesn't complete assignments? Is a child "immature" because he plays with toys in class? Is a child "bad" because he calls others names? Once you've identified the behavior, work with the teacher to correct it. The "lazy" child may need to have oral directions rephrased. The "immature" child may only need his toys taken away. And the "bad" child may need sensitivity training and a behavior management program to eliminate his name calling.

158. Participate in school events.

Attend every school concert, science fair, and assembly program that you can possibly attend. Show your child that school activities are important and enjoyable to you, too.

159.

Encourage your child to talk about school.

Refrain from asking the ever-popular question, "What did you learn in school today?" You already know the answer to that one. Instead, be more specific. Ask, "What did you discuss in science class?" or "Tell me one exciting thing that happened today," or "What new assignments did you get?"

160. Praise your child every day.

Comments like "I really like that you fed the dog without being asked" or "You did a fine job of selecting matching clothes today" go a long way in boosting self-esteem.

Children with high self-esteem do better in school. You can boost your child's ego by giving legitimate praise and compliments. Kids do many things right every day. So, get into the habit of looking for the goodness in your child, and practice giving "high fives" often.

161. Encourage your child to explore new interests: music, dance, drawing, photography, archery, bowling, quilting, crafting, magic, chess.

Having at least one hobby or interest outside of school gives your child an opportunity to express creativity and have fun. If your child is having trouble finding something to occupy his free time, here are some suggestions.

Many schools sponsor after-school clubs that are free. Check with your child's teacher or principal to see what's offered. Some schools offer evening or Saturday morning recreation classes to school-aged students. You can also find courses offered by colleges, zoos, and parks that are relatively inexpensive. And, of course, the YMCA, boys' or girls' clubs, private schools, and tutors teach music, dance, gymnastics, etc.

162.
Encourage your child to join scouting, a church group, or a youth service organization.

Much learning takes place outside of school. Many organizations provide hands-on learning experiences that will take your child beyond the classroom into a whole new world of recreation and career exploration. Youth groups help bridge the transition from childhood to adolescence to young-adulthood. They introduce children to activities such as hiking, camping, crafting, animal husbandry, and volunteerism, while providing a structured framework of youth fellowship and peer leadership. Your child will grow socially and intellectually through participation in a youth service organization.

163. Encourage your child to join at least one after-school club.

Children who get involved socially in school often do better in school. Many schools offer activities other than sports. Not every child can make the basketball team, and cheerleading competition has become cutthroat. But do encourage your child to join at least one club. After-school activities are fun, and having fun in school-sponsored clubs makes school more enjoyable.

Ask your child's teacher or principal which activities are available, and help your child find one to try on for size. Many schools offer such clubs as chess, D.A.R.E., foreign language, S.A.D.D., history, science, computer, student council, newspaper, etc.

164.

Attend an intramural sports game with your child and sit next to him.

Parents go to the game to watch their child play. But what if your child isn't an athlete? Show off your school spirit by taking your child to see a game. Cut loose—stomp your feet on the bleachers. Be a real winner—drive a group of his friends to the game and home again.

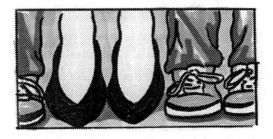

165. Limit television. Limit television. Limit television.

Ten hours per week for school-age children should do it.

166. Scrutinize your child's television viewing.

Sex, violence, and profanity are rampant, even on daytime TV. Is there a correlation between watching violence on TV and demonstrating more violent behaviors? Is the child who watches racy bedroom scenes on afternoon soaps more inclined to believe "everybody does it?" Will the child who listens to profanity on evening sitcoms curse more? The controversy rages on. But enough evidence has been gathered to coerce the television industry into flashing viewer ratings at the beginning of each program. That should tell us something.

Children who behave aggressively, curse excessively, and are preoccupied with sex don't do well in school. Monitor your child's television viewing. Watch your child's favorite programs at least once to determine if they meet your moral standards.

167.

Watch a program together on educational TV on a subject your child is learning in school.

There really is television beyond MTV. But chances are, your child won't discover educational networks on his own. You'll need to guide him. If you break the bedtime curfew rule, this will be a special treat. Be alert for programs that enhance your child's curriculum and watch them together. Then talk about them. Your child will garner better understanding of the subject than he would by simply reading the textbook.

168.
Declare a "No TV" night once a week and play family board games together instead.

Children who play board games learn how to take turns, make decisions, and develop sportsmanship. Here is a list of games with recommended ages and the skills they teach:

Name	Age Range	Skill Taught
Boggle	8–Adult	spelling, visual perception
Brain Quest	6–12	math, social studies, science, English
Candy Land	4–8	color recognition, counting, taking turns
Checkers	6–Adult	strategy, sportsmanship
Monopoly	8–Adult	money, finance, decision making
Scrabble	6–Adult	spelling, vocabulary
Trouble	5–Adult	number recognition, counting
Yahtzee	8–Adult	counting, addition

169. Visit a museum together and take the free one-hour tour.

Many large museums offer free tours. Climb aboard and watch your child walk away inspired and amazed.

Tours usually don't cover the entire museum. Instead, they focus on a particular section, historical period, or artist. One of the best things about tours are tour guides. They're smarter than pharaohs and more patient than monks. They focus your child's attention, point out minute details, and answer kazillions of questions. Kids (and adults) learn more from taking a one-hour tour than by wandering aimlessly about a large museum. And when a related topic comes up in school, your child will eagerly share her experience.

When you say the word *museum*, does your child shout, "BORING?" Remember, there are all kinds of museums:

Art: paintings, jewelry, marble sculptures, ancient toys
History: suits of armor, mummies, the Declaration of Independence
Natural History: tar pits, dinosaurs, reptiles, fish, birds, pterodactyls
Science and Technology: electricity, magnetism, machines, outer space

Children's and Youth: invite you to touch everything from frogs to computers

Zoos: lions and tigers and polar bears—oh my!

Aquariums: coral reefs, electric eels, wetlands, sharks

Special Interest: baseball, rock and roll, airplanes, trolley cars

Cultural Heritage: Native Americans, Native Hawaiians, Asians, African Americans, Hispanics

Botanical Gardens: exotic plants, glass houses, insect-eating plants, arboretums

Nature Centers: birds, bugs, butterflies

Planetariums: blast off to the moon, Mars, Saturn, the Milky Way

Restored Areas: Colonial Williamsburg, Old Sturbridge Village, mining towns

Historic Homes: George Washington, Jefferson Davis, FDR, Betsy Ross

170.

When on vacation, buy your child a book to remind her of your trip.

Bring home a souvenir that really comes in handy. Select a coloring book, a novel written by a local author, or nonfiction about the history of the area. During your child's school career, she'll need to talk and write about vacations, trips, and historical places. Souvenir shops are great resources. But if your child is like mine, chances are she won't bolt through the gift shop door heading straight for the book section. After all, plastic swords, flashy key chains, and tiny cedar boxes are too irresistible to pass by. So I've set two rules.

First, I pay for all books, even though my son spends his own money on souvenirs. Second, if he doesn't choose a book, I buy one anyway. Eventually, he'll use it for a school report. In the meantime, we relive our vacation by reading a book with a local tie-in or by coloring pictures of places visited.

171. Plan a family outing that reinforces what your child is learning in school.

This could be a trip to the state capital, a visit to a Civil War battlefield, or a safari to the zoo. Don't forget to buy a book while you're there.

"Good morning children. Today we are going to learn about colonial Philadelphia. Who can tell me something about Philadelphia during the Revolutionary War?"

"Benjamin Franklin lived there. I saw his printing press when we went to Philadelphia last summer."

"I saw the Liberty Bell when my family visited there."

"We walked down those funny stone streets and saw the house where Betsy Ross sewed the first American flag."

"Philadelphia is where they signed the Declaration of Independence."

Nothing promotes class participation and enhances understanding more than real-life experiences. Children leap from their desks to share information in class. And they remember more and grasp new concepts easier when they have background experiences to build on. So find out what your child is studying in school and take a trip. Have fun—the learning will happen practically by itself.

172.
Encourage your child to keep a diary while on vacation.

If your child is old enough to write a sentence, he is old enough to keep a vacation diary. Try not to make it torturous, but encourage your child to write down something every day. He should begin each entry on a new page.

The fun part happens after you return home. You and your child will relive many happy memories as you paste snapshots and postcards onto the diary pages. Finish with a sturdy cover or place into a three-ring binder. Your child now has an attractive journal to share with family and friends.

Keeping a vacation diary not only enhances and maintains your child's writing skills, but also comes in mighty handy for that "What I Did on Summer Vacation" writing task that's bound to be assigned during the first week back to school.

173. Play lost-and-found in the car.

Your child will be asked to read maps in school. There's no better way of making this a meaningful activity than by practicing in the car. Give your child a road map and ask her to direct you to your destination.

Motivated to find Jay Leno's house while on vacation, my eleven-year-old navigated us through Beverly Hills using a celebrity "star map." I'll admit, we made more than one U-turn, but we laughed all the way, and my son emerged successful and proud of his accomplishment.

Map reading will benefit your child for a lifetime. So give your child a map and ask her to direct you to the neighborhood playground. She will surely enjoy the reward waiting at the end of the trip.

174. On road trips, play language games like "Twenty Questions."

Whether you're driving to the supermarket or trekking across the country, there's no better opportunity to expand your child's language skills than while he's a captive learner in the car.

Children with sophisticated language skills do better in school. Language games teach youngsters how to formulate questions and target answers appropriately. They also expand vocabulary and teach children to categorize information.

To play "Twenty Questions," first think of a specific answer that fits into a category (Disney World, for example). Then announce the category, "I am thinking of a place." Your child then asks questions that have only a yes or no response. "Is your place in our neighborhood?" If your child poses a question that is off target, such as, "Is this somebody we know?" point out how that doesn't fit the category. The object of the game is to discover the answer in twenty questions or less. Hopefully, one question you will avoid is "Are we there yet?"

175. Listen to books on tape or have a child read aloud in the car.

When packing the car, don't forget to take along a good children's book. By the time the radio has groaned out the latest pop tune for the tenth time, you'll be singing your own praises for remembering a good read-aloud.

An exciting story will hold the interest of everybody in the car, no matter the age range. That's because good children's authors do with words what Disney does with animation. So forget about counting milepost markers and Guernsey cows. Instead, reach for a good book or pop a story on tape into the cassette player and enjoy the ride.

176. Let your teenager balance your checkbook.

Stock market crash. Inflation. The Great Depression. Global economy. Wall Street. These are difficult concepts for junior and senior high school students to understand. Your child will gain a better understanding of economics by balancing the family checkbook. He might also learn not to ask, "Why can't we afford a new . . ."

177. Encourage your child to choose the best teachers and select challenging courses that will help him attain his post–high school goals.

Sometimes students are at the mercy of a computer-generated schedule, but don't allow your child to select "cake" courses just to make senior year a breeze. The best way to get ready for college is by getting ready—now.

178.

Encourage your child to search out post–high school options before entering senior year.

Researching schools, filing applications, visiting campuses, and making decisions takes months. Whether your child is considering an Ivy League school, a community college, a trade school, the armed services, the Peace Corps, or going directly into the work force, she will feel more comfortable with her decision when given sufficient time to make her selection.

Visiting trade schools and colleges makes for enjoyable side trips while on family vacations. Schedule enough time to visit the admissions office, talk with students (they'll tell you what campus life is really like), and attend a sporting event or student activity.

179. Put the Scholastic Aptitude Test (SAT) in perspective.

While SAT scores do count, most college admissions personnel look for students who earned good grades in challenging high school courses. Rigorous academic preparation over time is the key to success on the SAT and in college. You may choose to spend money for SAT preparation courses, but their effect is dubious. SAT scores rise and fall for both coached and uncoached students. So how should your child prepare for the SAT? Here are some tips:

1. Take the Preliminary Scholastic Aptitude Test/National Merit Scholarship Qualifying Test (PSAT/NMSQT). With questions similar to the SAT, this is a good way to practice and get feedback.
2. Know the directions. The more time your child spends reading directions, the less time he'll have to answer the questions.
3. Answer the easy questions first. For the most part, the easier questions are at the beginning of each section and the harder questions are at the end. Your child will earn just as many points for answering the easy questions as hard questions.

4. Know how the test is scored. Your child will earn one point for each correct answer but will lose a fraction of a point for a wrong answer in most sections. No points are lost for unanswered questions.

180.

Plan ahead. Build a financial nest egg so your child can attend a college of choice.

You shouldn't be the only person stashing away money for college. Your working teenager needs to build a bankroll to help pay living and recreation expenses. But let's face it, the brunt of the responsibility falls on you.

Just how much money you'll need depends on many factors: the type of college your child attends, the amount of financial aid she is eligible for, the number of scholarships, grants, and awards received, and your personal net worth. Don't deny your child a college education because you think you can't afford it. According to 1998–99 figures collected by the College Board, over half (52.2 percent) of the students who attend four-year colleges go to institutions that charge less than $4,000 in tuition and fees. There are many resources to help finance a college education.

With prudent saving and careful planning, you can build a financial package that will enable your child to succeed in college.

For more information contact:

- U.S. Department of Education. 1-800-USA-LEARN. www.ed.gov
- Federal Student Aid Information Center. 1-800-433-3243
- The College Board. www.collegeboard.org